Kenan Kaya

ARGE – construction partnership in Germany

legal issues in cooperation of different engineering firms

Anchor Academic
Publishing

Kaya, Kenan: ARGE – construction partnership in Germany: legal issues in cooperation of different engineering firms. Hamburg, Diplomica Verlag GmbH 2012

ISBN: 978-3-95489-026-2
Print: Anchor Academic Publishing, an Imprint of Diplomica® Verlag GmbH, Hamburg, 2012

Bibliographical Information of the German National Library:
The German National Library lists this publication in the German National Bibliography.
Detailed bibliographic data can be found at: http://dnb.d-nb.de

The digital publication (eBook) of this work with the ISBN 978-3-95489-526-7 can be purchased on the general market or directly from the publisher.

I Executive Summary

This survey investigates and evaluates the legal framework for engineering firms to step into an ARGE partnership with other planning offices. ARGE, in German construction industry an established form of partnership, becomes more and more important in acquiring and accomplishing construction projects. Principals are interested in placing orders to ARGE partnerships, so they force it in tender procedures.

Reasons therefore are that the ARGE underlies the regulations of the German Partnership under Civil Law. Consequently the ARGE partners are jointly and several liable for the contract to produce a work with the principal. Thus the principal reaches fundamental advantages: He reduces his risk concerning insolvency of an ARGE partner, he increases competition and he gets services from one hand.

Engineering firms, who want to participate in these projects, have to handle their capacities and risks. Engineering firms are not interested in participating in ARGE partnerships. There is no reason for voluntary sharing of liability. Engineering firms want to be responsible and liable only for services they accomplish. They do not want to share the responsibility and liability with other construction planners.

Therefore engineering firms are interested in an ARGE agreement which divides the responsibilities and liabilities considering the rendered services. In external relationship with the principal, ARGE partners could not change the jointly and several liability. Principals will not deal about limitation of ARGE partners' liability. However in internal arrangements could be defined other regulations.

The ARGE model contract for building contractors, published by German Construction Industry Federation, could be adapted partly to the interests of engineering firms. From Chamber of Architects Baden-Württemberg published model contract is more suitable, because of equal treatment in liability and payment.

Beside the contract with the principal is the partnership agreement equally important. The ARGE agreement has to define the purpose of the partnership, the bodies of the partnership with their responsibilities and the services the partners have to accomplish for the ARGE. Partners have to be careful concerning liability. Partners should ensure in internal relationship that they are only responsible for services they had accomplished.

It is advisable to define other regulations in the ARGE agreement than the terms in law. For example, partners should define a fulfilment obligation, due to claim for damages by the principal. In case of insolvency of one partner, the other partners have still to fulfil the contract with the principal. If there are services they cannot carry out by themselves, they have to integrate other partners.

Engineering firms have to weigh within the framework of their business risk, if they are interested in acquiring the contract under the precondition to participate in an ARGE partnership. Capacity utilization is just important as the choice of partner.

II Table of Contents

I Executive Summary

III List of Abbreviations

AO	The Fiscal Code of Germany
ARGE	German Construction Partnership
BBR	Special insurance conditions and risk characterisation for professional liability insurance for Architects and Engineers
BeGe	Assistance Partnership in German Construction Industry
BGB	German Civil Code
BGH	Federal Court of Justice
BiGe	Bidding Consortium
CEO	Chief executive officer
EStG	German Income Tax Act
et seq.	and the following pages
EUR	Euro
GbR	Legal form in Germany: Partnership under Civil Law
GewStG	German Commercial Law Act
GmbH	Limited Liability Company
HOAI	Fee Structure for Architects and Engineers
HVAC	Heating ventilation and air condition
Ibid	ibidem / the same
ICT	IT networks, communication lines and telephones
InsO	Insolvency Statute of Germany
no.	number

URL	Uniform Resource Locator
VOB	German Contract Construction Procedures
VOF	Procedures for supply and services of Freelancers
ZPO	Code of Civil Procedure in Germany

IV List of Figures

1 Introduction

Partnerships between construction companies become more and more important in accomplishment of large construction projects. Companies, who want to participate in large projects, have to handle their capacities and risks. Principals have their own interests: they are interested in increasing the competition, they want services from one hand and they also want to reduce their risks

Engineering firms are also affected. How can small and mid-sized engineering firms acquire and accomplish large construction projects? There are different forms of partnership to enhance the capabilities and to fulfil the competition requirements.

Facing the competition requirements, the construction branch in Germany has established the partnership form of ARGE[1]. This partnership is a special construction cooperation in Germany. It is widely recognized in partnerships between contractors and is legally supported[2]. The ARGE partnership form is also supported by a model contract published by German Construction Industry Federation. The Chamber of Architects in Baden – Württemberg have also drafted a model contract for architects.

However, competitive conditions often pose high hurdles in Germany. Tenderer have to show their capability by disclosure of references, number of employees, office equipment and especially in procedures for supply and services of freelancers (VOF), they have to verify the professional experience of their employees.

Additionally, there are tenders which expect the foundation of an ARGE for example for architecture and engineering services[3].

Engineering firms are not interested in accepting liability for services they are not competent for. Considering the principal, there are different interests which have to be coupled.

[1] ARGE – in literature ARGE is defined contradictory. For example, on the website of Hochtief the term of "ARGE - Arbeitsgemeinschaft" is defined as consortium (http://www.hochtief.com/hochtief_en/117.jhtml, date 29.01.2012) In the model contract for ARGE -agreement of Hauptverband der Deutschen Bauindustrie e.V. ARGE is translated as „Joint Venture". In German the term "ARGE – Arbeitsgemeinschaft" is used as one time cooperation for one project. To prevent confusion the term "ARGE" is not translated and used in German language as fixed term.

[2] Heiermann, W. et al. (2008), page 155.

[3] http://ted.europa.eu/udl?uri=TED:NOTICE:42398-2012:TEXT:DE:HTML&src=0, date: 08.02.2012.

In this survey will be discussed and illustrated the legal relations and difficulties of ARGE partnerships between engineering firms. Reflection starts with contractual relationships in the construction industry and the linkage to the Fee Structure for Architects and Engineers (HOAI). After that there was an overview about the ARGE structure, continued with screening the formal start – up requirements.

The main part of the book is divided in internal and external relationship. Liability and responsibility are the main terms which would be investigated in relation to principal and ARGE partners. After showing up the restriction possibilities considering insolvency of an ARGE partner or non-performing partners, the study comes to the end with an overview about tax matters.

The survey was accomplished by starting in desk research, continuing in literature research and verification in jurisdiction. To get a practical relevance there were accomplished interviews with a CEO of an engineering firm[4] and an interview with a tax consultant[5].

[4] Müller & Bleher Filderstadt GmbH & Co. KG.
[5] Ellinger & Rückle Steuerberatungsgesellschaft Partnerschaft.

2 Problem Definition

Usually there are different persons involved in the construction of a building. There are the principal, who could be the building owner or investor, the architect, planners and building contractors. Architects and planners are assigned by the building owner to consult him and to consider building laws and technical regulations. Architects and planners act on behalf of the principal on the construction site. Based on this frame conditions, they are practically the contact persons for contractors and building authorities.

Planners are employed in engineering firms. In Germany there are more than 35.000[6] engineering firms for building services. They are responsible for the different parts of the technical systems within the building. In general, the services are divided in mechanical engineering and electrical engineering. The majority of the companies only offer one of the before mentioned services.

Many builders expect to have one contractor for consulting and planning the building services. Therefore many companies organized themselves by commissioning or subcontracting the missing half. However, subcontracting can also be problematic. First of all, subcontracts are independent of the main contract. The principal has no contractual access to the subcontractor. One example from market is a constellation which is common and wide spread: an engineering office for HVAC – Systems has none specialist for electrical systems, in consequence they have to engage an engineering firm for the electrical engineering. Nevertheless there may come up difficulties in the construction phase. For example the contractor for the electrical system may deliver and install the wrong devices. Because of bad construction site management the subcontracted engineering firm for electrical systems is involved. Due to the main contract between building owner and engineering firm for HVAC - systems they are also involved.

[6] Federal Statistical Office Germany (2011), page 15.

Additionally there could arise some more problems at the end of the project. The acceptance and handover of the building is difficult in two ways, on the one hand due to the handover from the subcontractor to the main contractor and on the other hand due to the handover from the main contractor to the building owner. It could be that the subcontractor has finished his work earlier than the main contractor and wants to accomplish the acceptance in order to issue his final invoice.

Another problem could come up when the builder runs into financial difficulties and is not able to bring up the project costs, which leads to insecurities with regards to the overall project funding. In this case the subcontractor could only deal with his contracting entity. These described problems are not minor losses. On the construction site all parts of constructing a building are closely linked to each other. That means that the end date for the hand over to the builder could be delayed and cause significantly higher costs. At this point, mistakes become very expensive. And due to the contractual constellation – the engineering firm for HVAC – Systems is also involved.

A possible solution for remediation could be an ARGE. In Germany ARGE is known as a partnership between contractors for large construction projects which cannot be accomplished solely by one contractor. Organizing engineering firms in ARGE cooperation like contractors do could be a better instrument in working relationship for construction projects. The partners of the ARGE would then have a direct contract with the building owner.

Nevertheless an ARGE contract also incorporates risks and difficulties. There are internal and external regulations which to be taken into consideration. For example there could come up problems with external authorization, internal and external rights and obligations of the ARGE partners. But also more difficult problems like the situation when one partner of the ARGE could not fulfill his contract by less service provision. Another question is: How to cope with the insolvency of one ARGE partner?

The main problem for engineering firms in ARGE partnerships is that they are jointly and severally liable with other partners. Engineering firms want to handle or limit their share in liability[7].

---

[7] Müller, M. (2012), Interview.

Literature is more focused on ARGE for contractors. Special literature for ARGE of engineering firms is not available. The regulations must be adapted to engineering firms, but not all subjects can be transferred. Engineering firms underlie different laws and regulations than contractors[8].

[8] Krause-Allenstein, F. (2007), page 618.

3 Contract relationships in construction projects

3.1 Contract to produce a work and service contract

Architecture and engineering contracts are not specifically regulated In German Civil Code[9]. The German Civil Code regulates two relevant types of contracts: the contract to produce a work[10] and the service contract. Construction, planning and consulting contracts, can be adapted to these in BGB legal regulated contract forms. The coherency to the German Civil Code is necessary to have a legal basis.

The service contract is defined in section 611 et seq. of BGB and the contract to produce a work is defined in section 631 et seq. of BGB[11]. The two types differ fundamentally from each other, so it is very important to choose the correct type of contract.

Contract to produce a work leads engineering firms to a success-oriented, strict liability to develop a property free of defects[12]. In contrast to contract for services the warranty period for buildings is five years[13]. Contract to produce a work has a wide range of applications in construction. All kinds of contractual cooperation are involved, also technical systems which are integrated in the building according to sections 93 and 94 of BGB[14].

Construction is a development and realisation process, which the engineer has to accompany with planning and site management. So the work he has to produce develops during the construction realisation. So there are also elements of service contracts. But in German law they were consistently treated like contracts to produce a work[15].

---

[9] Wirth, A. et al. (2004), page 47.

[10] The German legal term „Werkvertrag" is translated in a variety of ways. For example in the Langenscheidt Routledge Technical Dictionary (3rd edition, 2007) is the legal term translated as „service contract" or „works contract". In Fidic – An Analysis of International Construction Contracts, the legal term is translated as „Contract for works". In this book is used the legal term of „Contract to produce a work" inspired by the official translation of the German Civil Code.

[11] Mütze, M. et al. (2007), page 129.

[12] OLG Frankfurt (1981): Judgement from 27.05.1981 – 17 U 82/80, in BauR 1983, 156.

[13] BGB (2009), section 634.

[14] BGH (1997): Judgement from 15.05.1997 – VII ZR 287 /95, in BauR 1997, 1018.

[15] Häußermann, D. et al (2008), page 27.

A contract for services does not contain any liability for success and does not include the claim for supplementary performance[16]. Example for service contract is the treatment contract with the doctor. The doctor does not promise the healing, he does promise the proper treatment. Considering the construction branch, service contracts, have no obligations to carry out an acceptance. So the builder has no possibility to find out if the work was completed according to the specifications and rules[17].

An engineering firm owes not the construction of a building as a physical object. The engineering firm is obligated for a faultless planning and if appropriate the construction supervision according to the rules[18].

As described, architects and engineers contracts are not defined as independently contract in German Civil Code. In prevailing case law engineers contract have to be assigned as contract to produce a work[19]. Objective of the contracts is the building of a structure.

[16] URL: http://www.brennecke-partner.de/48530/Der-Architekten--und-Ingenieurvertrag-als-Werkvertrag, date: 20.11.2011.
[17] Wirth, A. et al. (2004), page 47.
[18] Häußermann, D. et al (2008), page 27.
[19] Simmendinger, H. (2009), page 1.

3.2 Architecture and Engineering relationships

There are different contractual opportunities available to link the partners of a construction project. The builder could bind each partner with separate contracts. He could also only engage a general planner which offers all necessary planning services. In the most cases are many companies and people are involved in the construction of a building. For example the principal or client can be the owner who will use the building or an investor who wants to lease or sell the building. The principal will usually always try to get the best quality coupled with the minimum price. So there are many options to order a building in Germany. This book is focused on realizing a building by involvement of architects and planners, who are responsible for planning and supervising.

In Figure 1 is shown a general example for contractual relationships in construction.

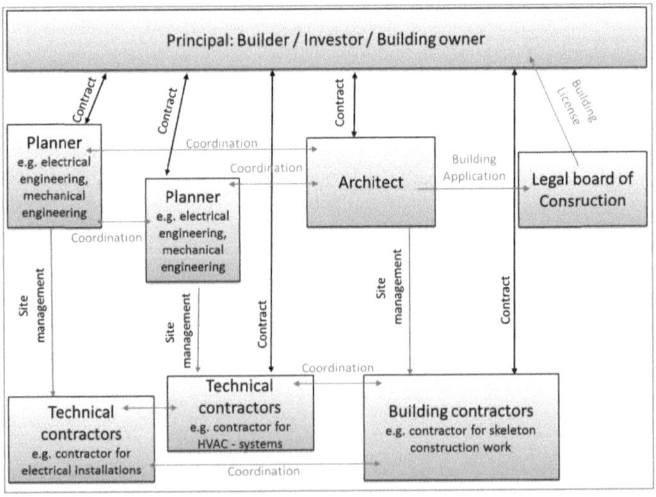

Figure 1: Relationships in construction projects[20]

The principal has direct contracts with all partners which are involved in accomplishing the building project. The planners and architects are not only responsible for planning and supervising their trades, they also have the obligation of coordinating with each

[20] According to: Häußermann, D. et al. (2008), page 14.

other. Technical contractors also have the obligation for coordination with each other and with the building contractor. In general the planners and architects have to work together with the executing company on behalf of the principal. Furthermore the architect is responsible to reach the building license for the construction project.

In this model has the principal contractual relationship with each of the construction partners. To simplify the project management on his side and to handle responsibilities and liabilities for accomplishing services, the principal is interested in bundling services. So he could bundle packages which fit to each other, like the building services, or for example the whole planning procedure.

Planners could join together for one construction project in terms of an ARGE. In Figure 2 is shown a possible contractual constellation with participation of an ARGE for building services.

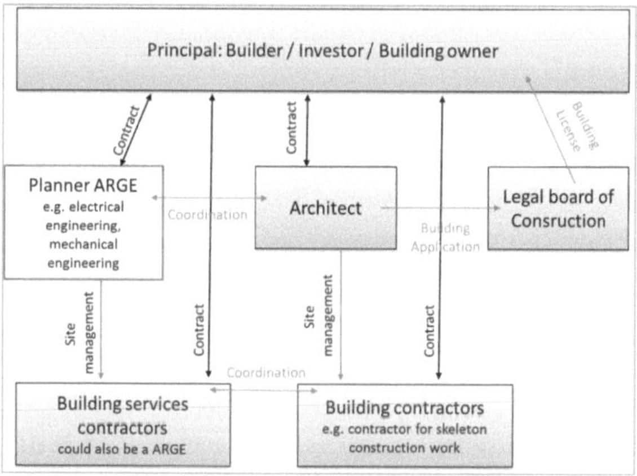

Figure 2: Contractual relationship with ARGE[21]

In this case the engineering firms for planning building services are centralized in the ARGE. The builder has only one contract for engineering the building services. As described, the contract form between the builder or investor and the ARGE for engineering is defined in the German Civil Code as contract to produce a work. This contract form is the most used contract form for construction projects.

[21] According to: Häußermann, D. et al. (2008), page 14.

Payment to each partner is regulated in the several contracts. References for payments to architecture and engineering firms are regulated in the HOAI.

3.3 Linkage to HOAI

The HOAI is a Fee Structure for Architects and Engineers, which allows calculating the remuneration based on the cost calculation of each trade. So the objective of the HOAI is to provide a calculation method to assist parties without fee agreement. Furthermore the prescribed calculating method is an instrument, to proof the remuneration agreement. It can be verified if the fixed fee is within the maximum and minimum rate[22].

The HOAI couples the ordered service to the scope of work. Scope of work is defined in the HOAI[23], where does not contain any information standardised by law on the content or scope of an engineer's contract[24]. In legal practice engineering services are assigned to contracts to produce a work[25].

The HOAI is divided in services. Services which will be aligned have to be defined in the contract to produce a work between the engineering firm and the principal[26]. The BGH has confirmed, that it is allowed to define services by reference to HOAI[27].

If the contract to produce a work contains only several parts from the HOAI, for example the service phase 8 – construction supervising, than the contract is also defined as contract to produce a work[28]. According to the conviction of BGH[29] the scope of works, which are defined in the HOAI, could serve as a basis in the contract. Restriction is that the scope of work has to be mentioned in the contract.

---

[22] Locher, H. et al. (2010), page 407.
[23] Häußermann, D. et al. (2008), page 35.
[24] Mütze, M. et al. (2007), page 127.
[25] Locher, H. et al. (2010), page 407.
[26] Häußermann, D. et al. (2008), page 35.
[27] http://www.baunetz.de/recht/BGH_bestaetigt_Bezugnahme_auf_Leistungsbilder_oder_Leistungsphasen_der_HOAI_fuehrt_zu_entsprechender_Leistungspflicht_44766.html, date: 27.01.2012.
[28] BGH (1974): Judgement from 07.03.1974 - VII ZR 217/72, in BGHZ 62, 204.
[29] BGH (2007): Judgement from 26.07.2007 - V II ZR 42 / 05, in BGHZ 173, 314.

Section 7 of the HOAI does not affect employment relationships. So Engineers and Architects, who have an employment contract with their employers or instruction dependent freelancers, have not the HOAI as their legal basis[30]. In this case the HOAI can only be utilized as basis for interpretation.

HOAI payment agreements are often used for determination of shareholding in the ARGE. So in ARGE agreements, there can be a reference to the contract to produce a work. In this contract with the principal is defined the payment to the ARGE. Also could be linked the ownership-share ratio of the ARGE to the contract for work and services.

Partners of ARGE have to be ensuring to separate their services strictly horizontal. In this case the HOAI could be involved in the ARGE agreement. Payment could be coupled to the accomplishment of services.

[30] BGH (1999): Judgement from 12.07.1999 - II ZR 4/98, in BauR 1999, 1471.

3.4 General planner

As described before, many engineering firms and architects assign subcontracts with other firms in order to offer the entire planning service. This instrument, to meet the builder's needs, to reach all services from one hand, is called general planner[31]. However there are many difficulties which are coupled with subcontracts. For example the builder has no direct contractual relationship with subcontracted companies[32].

According to the phases of the HOAI, the general planning contract could obtain different performances. For example can be instructed the object planning and the outside facilities. The same applies to the structure planning and sound insulation verification.

With subcontracts engages the general planner the appropriate consultants and engineering firms. The engineering firms have only contractual relationship with the general planner. The risks are apparent: the general planner has far reaching liability risks. He is liable for faulty planning of his subcontractors.

If subcontractors have not sufficient liability insurance, the general planner has no chances of success with a claim for compensation. The general planner has to close a liability insurance contract which covers the risks with subcontractors. A usual architect cannot act as a general planner, his liability insurance covers him not against losses which occur through subcontractors[33].

Also a disadvantage is to sign up a contract which contains minimum rates of HOAI fee structure. The general planner has to invoice individual subcontracts. According to HOAI, the single contracts fees are higher than the remuneration for the overall contract[34].

Reason therefore is that the HOAI is digressive - single contracts in the sum are higher than the overall contract. One more disadvantage is the risk for the general planner that

---

[31] Wirth, A. et al. (2004), page 37.
[32] Gauch, P. (1982), page 155 .
[33] Wirth, A. et al. (2004), page 37.
[34] Wirth, A. et al. (2004), page 37.

he has to pay his subcontractors although he was not paid by the client. Risks can be reduced by terms in subcontractor contracts[35].

For engineering firms, is the preferred contractual position, the position of the subcontracted company[36]. As subcontractor, the engineering firm has a clearly defined scope of services to accomplish. Liability is delimited just the same. On the other side, for general planners is the ARGE useful. They are used to be liable for all services. In an ARGE partnership they could share the liability.

[35] Ibid., page 37.
[36] Müller, M. (2012), Interview.

4 Purpose and types of ARGE between engineering firms

4.1 Purpose of ARGE

In building practice many contractors need partners in accomplishing construction projects. Partnership is not only necessary because of the size of the construction site. There are also technical, economic and organisational reasons.

First of all capacity or manpower is a reason to set up a partnership. Coupled with this reason is the time pressure of investors, who want to accomplish projects in shorter construction time. Specialized sole proprietorships have also reason to form partnerships. They need partners to offer entire services. Sole proprietorships and small companies have to face difficulties in entering the bidding process for large construction projects. They need partners to show that they are inclined to accomplish successful the contract to produce a work[37]. Companies have to be aware of their solvency and flexibility according to their business activities[38]. Size of contract should not commit the whole company and should not exceed companies' capacity.

According to section 6 of German Contract Construction Procedures (VOB) part A, bidding consortiums are equal to all other bidders. In this context ARGE partnerships are supported, due to partnership of mid-sized companies the competition will be higher[39]. Certainly must be mentioned, that VOB part B cannot be agreed in engineering contracts[40]. So the VOB as German Construction Contract Procedures have no influence in engineering contracts.

On the one hand an ARGE partnership increases the solvency and capacity of the partners; on the other hand the economic risk will be shouldered by partners[41]. As described in the previous chapter, ARGE is a useful partnership for general planners. General planners are responsible for the entire services. With the ARGE the partners have also to shoulder the liability.

---

[37] Jagenburg, I.; Schröder, C. U. (2008), page 11.
[38] Bärwaldt, R. (2002), page 1101.
[39] Heiermann, W. et al. (2008), page 155.
[40] Wirth, A. et al. (2004), page 47.
[41] Bärwaldt, R. (2002)., page 1101 .

Additional reasons for engineering companies are pre-financing and liability. Usually they are required to finish a phase according to HOAI before they get a payment.

There are also advantages for the principal. One important advantage for the builder or investor is the reduction of risk. If one member of the ARGE could not fulfil his part or becomes insolvent, the other members have to fill out the space and are still in duty to complete the project work[42]. From the principals point of view, the ARGE simplifies administrative and coordination expenses.

[42] Ibid., page 1102.

4.2 Types of ARGE

There are mainly two types of ARGE: the horizontal ARGE and the vertical ARGE. The horizontal ARGE is the widely recognized form of ARGE. The partners provide services to accomplish the project. The partners could have different focusses on performance. In picture 3 is shown the constellation of horizontal ARGE.

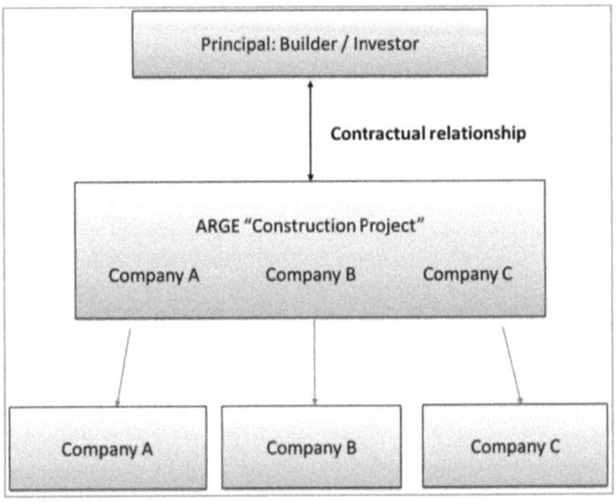

Figure 3: Horizontale ARGE[43]

In this example the ARGE consists of three partners. For example company A could be the engineering firm for planning the electrical systems, company B could be the engineering firm for HVAC – Systems, and company C could be the planner for the sprinkler system.

The builder has a contract with the ARGE which was founded by three companies. The three partners have to provide, manpower, machines, etc. All members are jointly responsible ·for accomplishing the project. The contractual relationship within the ARGE is not important for the principal; he gets all services from one hand.

In the ARGE agreement has to be defined which kind of capacities, contributions and performances the partners have to bring into the ARGE. In this case, the capacities will

[43] According to Messerschmidt, B.; Thierau, T. (2007a), page 9.

be technical and specialised knowledge, manpower and deposit to start working the ARGE.

The other type of ARGE or a variation of ARGE[44] is the so called Dach-ARGE or vertical ARGE. In external relationship there is no differentiation between horizontal and Dach-ARGE. Internal arrangements specify that that the services of the Dach-ARGE have to be divided into smaller packages. This smaller package will be subcontracted from the Dach-ARGE to each of the partners as subcontractor. All construction services will be accomplished by subcontracting the Dach-ARGE members. The Dach-ARGE does not accomplish direct services, but one possible task could be the responsibility for coordination.

Thus in internal relationship the partners are not liable for the complete service which the Dach-ARGE has to deliver, they are only responsible and liable for the subcontracted part[45]. So this type of Dach-ARGE supports only the exactly separation of the performance. Claims for defects could be addressed to the affected partner easier. This type will be founded when different partners yield different services[46], and when the services could be precisely differentiated. The structure of Dach-ARGE is shown in picture 4.

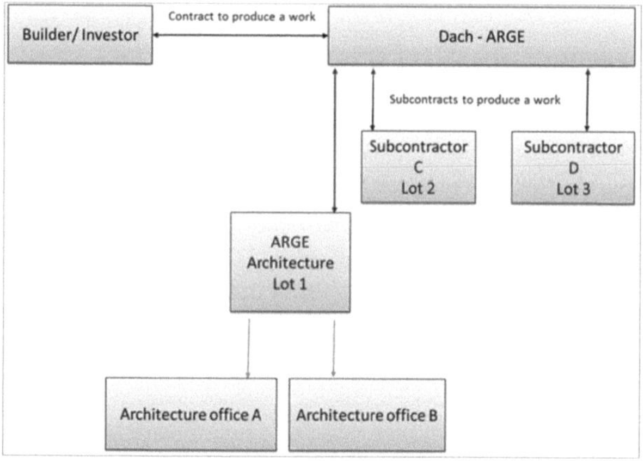

Figure 4: Structure of Dach-ARGE[47]

[44] Palandt, O.; Sprau, Hartwig (2008), section 705 marginal no. 37.
[45] Messerschmidt B.; Thierau, T. (2007b), page 3.
[46] Karl, S. (2007), page 636.
[47] According to http://bwi-bau.de/fileadmin/daten/pdf/Argeformen.pdf., date 05.02.2012.

In Dach-ARGE, partners have a dual role. On one hand they are subcontractor of the Dach-ARGE with all his duties and obligations, and on the other hand they are shareholder of the ARGE[48]. Due to his position as shareholder, the partner has to fulfil his duty of allegiance towards the other partners[49]. This duty goes beyond the common subcontract. Nevertheless each partner is full liable for the hole Dach-ARGE. So the liability in relation to the principal is the same as in an ordinary ARGE[50].

Disadvantage is still, that in case of insolvency of one partner, the other partners have to fulfil the contract with the principal - independent from the type of ARGE. The type of Dach-ARGE is useful to separate the service according to the partners. However the services from engineering firms could be clearly differentiated according to HOAI.

However there is coupled a higher administrative effort for the Dach-ARGE, because of separate subcontracts which have to be signed and recognized. Each partner will have two contracts: The contract with the principal, which is the same for all partners, and the individual contract with the Dach-ARGE. Contracts have to be congruent otherwise there result gaps in services, which could lead the Dach-ARGE in difficulties.

5 Legal forms of ARGE

5.1 Basic legal form of ARGE: Partnership under Civil Law

The regular legal form of ARGE cooperation is the Partnership under Civil Law. The partnership under Civil Law is also called Civil Law Association and will be abbreviated in Germany as GbR[51]. The partnership is regulated in section 705 et seq. of BGB.

Architects and Engineers are freelancers. They are not accomplishing commercial trade, so the suitable legal form for partnerships of them is Partnership under Civil Law.

[48] Jagenburg, I.; Schröder, C. U. (2008), page 40.
[49] Ibid, page 40.
[50] Ibid., page 40.
[51] http://www.existenzgruender.de/selbstaendigkeit/vorbereitung/gruendungswissen/rechtsform/05/index.php, date 07.02.2012.

Disadvantage for the partners of the Partnership under Civil Law is that they are jointly and several liable in relation to the principal[52].

The Partnership under Civil Law is the basic form of all partnerships. It consists of at least two small traders carrying out a business together[53]. Foundation regulations are very simple; therefore this is one of the reason why this legal form is so popular as regulation for ARGE agreements. The Partnership under Civil Law is a partnership of persons based on a partnership agreement without legal entity. Important for this legal form is the "duty to promote the achievement of a common purpose"[54]. Transferred to the ARGE agreement – the accomplishment of a construction project will be the mutual purpose.

Partners of a Partnership under Civil Law can be each natural persons or legal entities[55]. Agreements can be reached by written partnership agreements, but also tacitly and implied[56].

As a non-trading partnership, an ARGE is not a firm according to HGB[57]. As HGB the partnership has to consider different additional regulations, for example accounting, and registration in commercial registration. The partnership assets are part of the assets of the partners. There is no minimum capital required for setting up the Partnership under Civil Law.

Typical characteristics of Partnership under Civil Law are that the partners are jointly and severally liable[58]. Third parties are able to place claims against each of the individual partners. GbR has a legal capacity[59].

The partners have the duty of encouragement of a shared purpose by performing contributions[60]. The partners themselves are not merchants. The partnership assets are liable for the partnership debts just as all partners are liable personally and without restriction with their private assets as joint and several debtors.

---

52 Bärwaldt, R. (2002), page 1102.
53 http://www.frankfurt-main.ihk.de/english/business/legal_forms/gbr/, date: 31.12.2011.
54 BGB (2009), section 705.
55 Giefers, H.-W.; Ott, H. (2000), page 56.
56 Hueck, G.; Windbichler, C. (2008), page 46.
57 Jagenburg, I.; Schröder, C. U. (2008), page 12.
58 Lang, F. et al. (2010), page 133.
59 BGH (2001): Judgement from 29.01.2001 – II ZR 331/00, in NJW 2001, 1056.
60 Bärwaldt, R. (2002), page 1102.

The members of a Partnership under Civil Law are not necessary subject to social security contributions, for example pension insurance, health insurance and unemployment insurance[61].

A partnership under Civil Law could be an inward turned partnership or an outward turned partnership[62]. The difference between the two types is that the inward turned partnership is not obvious for outside third parties, because one of the partners appears outside the partnership alone[63]. In case of outward turned partnership several persons or partners perform as representative and authorized signatory. In the case of inward turned partnership there is only one person or partners who have authority to represent the Partnership under Civil Law. The inward turned partnership does not act externally in legal[64]. This form of partnership could also be used for coordination purposes, without a third party is aware of existence of the partnership[65]. Business transaction will be accomplished by one partner. Only the external management has legal capacity[66].

Generally accepted for differentiation between the two partnership-types: If management acts on his own behalf to fulfil the purpose of the partnership, it has to be an undisclosed partnership - if he represents recognizable a partnership, than it is an outward turned partnership[67].

Reflected on ARGE partnerships, in the ARGE contract must be defined in which form the partners want to regulate the representation of the ARGE. As long as the contract defines nothing else, partners are "jointly entitled to manage the business of the partnership; for each transaction the approval of all partners is required"[68].

The characteristic of an ARGE partnership differs from the Partnership under Civil Law[69]. According to legal requirements, partners have to define other regulations which differ from law[70]. However there are also regulations which have to be fulfilled strictly. ARGE partners could not differ from these regulations in the ARGE agreement. For example, ARGE agreement could not define a regulation which excludes a partner from

[61] http://www.frankfurt-main.ihk.de/english/business/legal_forms/gbr/, date: 31.12.2011.
[62] Giefers, H.-W.; Ott, H. (2000), page 50.
[63]Giefers, H.-W.; Ott, H. (2000), page 50.
[64] Jagenburg, I.; Schröder, C. U. (2008), page 37.
[65] http://bgb.jura.uni-hamburg.de/av/gesellschaftsrecht/bgb-g.htm, date: 06.01.2012.
[66] Jagenburg, I.; Schröder, C. U. (2008)., page 37.
[67] http://bgb.jura.uni-hamburg.de/av/gesellschaftsrecht/bgb-g.htm, date 06.01.2012.
[68] BGB (2009): section 709.
[69] Bärwaldt, R. (2002), page 1103.
[70] Burchardt, H.-P., Pfülb, W. (1998), page 115.

his right of control and right for information's according to section 716 of BGB. Equally will be definitions inoperative, which exclude the right of termination the partnership according to section 723 of BGB.

Transfer of corporate share is not clearly described in law. The ARGE model contracts also did not mention it. There could be two ways of a shareholder exchange. One possibility is that the new shareholder bargains with the other shareholders and the moment of leaving and entering the ARGE are the same. The second way could be the assignment of interests. The exiting partner transfers his share to the entering partner[71]. According to section 1069 and 1274 of BGB is usufruct on shares only possible when the shares are representing transferable rights[72].

In ARGE agreements for architects and engineers should be restricted the possibility to transfer the shares. Reasons therefore are that this form of partnership entails joint and severally liability. And partners have signed a contract to fulfil the requirements. It is not in the interest of the ARGE member, when another partner transfers his share to a new partner and leaves the partnership.

[71] Lang, F. et al. (2010), page 249.
[72] Ibid., page 249.

5.2 Other legal forms

In general the form of Partnership under Civil Law will be chosen, because of the simple start-up and closing modalities. However there are also other possible legal forms. For example there are other partnerships and the limited liability corporation.

As mentioned, the company with limited liability is also a possible legal form for ARGE cooperation. Considering that one construction project has to be realized, this legal form is coupled to enhanced administrative expenses and is excessive formalized in start-up procedure[73]. Founding a company with limited liability is also coupled with high start-up costs[74]. ARGE partners have also to consider, that they have to accomplish a yearly balance sheet. Partners have to be concerning about the restrictive year after closing the limited liability[75]. The restrictive year serve the creditor protection. Furthermore, closing a limited liability is coupled to many restrictions, primarily caused by the removal from commercial register[76].

Partners have to be careful not to start up an OHG[77]. If one partner operates a commercial enterprise or the ARGE starts commercial trade, the ARGE becomes by law a commercial partnership[78]. This will have legal consequences which have to be considered: for example the ARGE must be listed in the commercial register. This registration has the consequences that partner which have leaved the ARGE are still liable according to section 15 of HGB, when their exit from the ARGE was not fixed in the commercial register. This applies also when the oHG was not registered, because the partners assumed that they are running a Partnership under Civil Law[79].

There are additional special regulations in commercial law. For example the ARGE has to maintain the accounting obligations like preparing a balance sheet. Finally there is not an exact definition in which case an ARGE becomes an oHG. However partners have to be careful and have to consider the legal form, which defines the legal

---

[73] Bärwaldt, R. (2002), page 1103.
[74] Kieß, D. (2012), Interview.
[75] Ibid., interview.
[76] http://www.stuttgart.ihk24.de/recht_und_fair_play/Gesellschaftsrecht_Unternehmensformen/Wahl_der_Rechtsform-Gesellschaftsrecht/971294/Aufloesung_GmbH.html;jsessionid=8B1E2A5DB441469EDF68A3D7C3C55376.repl23#8, date 07.02.2012.
[77] Jagenburg, I.; Schröder, C. U. (2008), page 12.
[78] Ibid., page 13.
[79] Ibid., page 32.

framework for their business dealings. In this context must also be considered, that the continuing – ARGE is always an oHG[80].

Another partnership is the BEGE cooperation. The BEGE is comparable with the ARGE partnership with one fundamental differentiation: the BEGE is an internal partnership without joint property. External management will be accomplished by contractor. In internal relationship he gets support from partners who reach remuneration[81].

Concerning that the partners are interested in achievement of profit and reducing tax burden, they will prefer Partnership under Civil Law. Further reasons are caused by principals, who demand jointly and several liability[82].

---

80 Schwarz, K. (2007), page 637.

81 Palandt, O.; Sprau, H. (2008), section 705 marginal no. 37.

82 http://ted.europa.eu/udl?uri=TED:NOTICE:28746-2012:TEXT:DE:HTML&src=0, date: 08.02.2012.

5.3 Differentiation from other coalitions

Contrary to common belief, the ARGE is not a Joint Venture[83]. In German linguistic a Joint Venture is a long-time partnership between companies to tap in emerging markets. A joint venture could be suitable for engineering firms, when the partners are interested in accomplishing projects in a foreign country for an indefinite time. There are many countries, who do not allow foreign companies to acquire projects or to open an establishment. Often they have to form a joint venture with a local partner[84].

For example, in United Arab Emirates it is necessary to enter a joint venture. The runtime of the joint venture is normally not limited. However joint ventures are unsuitable for accomplishing single projects[85].

On the other hand, in international linguistic usage a joint venture is a "commercial agreement between two or more companies in order to allow greater ease of work and cooperation towards achieving a common aim, through the manipulation of the appropriate resources"[86]. So the term joint venture is also used as cooperation in the construction industry for accomplishment of one individual construction project. However as described in Germany the term of joint venture is only used for cooperation between companies, which start up a new business unit[87]. So partners have to be careful with their foreign business partners, if they talk about the same legal form.

Another partnership is the consortium. The consortium has legal characteristics like an external GbR. The differentiation to the ARGE: partners of the consortium do not bring in contributions to fulfil an overall performance, but they fulfil their part of the performance self-dependent[88].

Profit and losses accrue not in the consortium. Each member gets a proportionate compensation for his work. Due to splitting profit and losses, there is also a risk-splitting in consortium. In contrast to ARGE partnerships: There is a risk-sharing[89].

[83] Burchardt, H.-P., Pfülb, W. (1998), page 611.
[84] http://guide.theemiratesnetwork.com/living/business.php, date 07.02.2012
[85] Devonshire-Ellis, C. et al (2011), page 4.
[86] Norwood, S. R.; Mansfield N. R. (1999), page 89.
[87] http://www.foerderland.de/2101.0.html, date: 29.12.2011.
[88] Jagenburg, I.; Schröder, C. U. (2008), page 43.
[89] Bärwaldt, R. (2002), page 1105.

Consortium is mainly used in financial economy[90]. In contrast to the ARGE has the consortium no corporate assets[91]. Also differing is the liability. Members are only liable for services they provide; they are not several liable like the partners in the ARGE[92].

[90] Ibid., page 1103.
[91] Jagenburg, I.; Schröder, C. U. (2008), page 43.
[92] Bärwaldt, R. (2002), page 1104.

6 Foundation of ARGE for engineering firms

As described is ARGE a short-term contractual cooperation between companies to accomplish one construction project within a period of time[93]. Usually the start-up of cooperation like the ARGE will be performed according to section 705 et seq. of BGB as a Partnership of Civil Law[94]. Therefore the following remarks are hit under the assumption that the ARGE will be started up under the legal form of Partnership under Civil Law.

Usually an ARGE starts as a bidding consortium[95]. In the case of order, the bidding consortium, in Germany also called BiGe will be continued as ARGE. The relationship between the ARGE partners will be regulated by an article of incorporation[96].

Commonly partners subscribe a pre-contract to reach ability to act[97]. The pre-contract defines the role of the partners in the bidding consortium and does not contain all details of an ARGE contract. An important part in the pre-contract is the mutual obligation to start-up an ARGE[98].

In general in Germany, companies have to be flexible to reach construction contracts. Advance performance has to be accomplished only for participation on a tender. In many tenders, principals are expecting the foundation of an ARGE in case of ordering[99].

To demonstrate the will of founding an ARGE, the partners of the BiGe have to hand in a declaration of the bidding consortium, which confirms the foundation of an ARGE in case of ordering[100].

In figure 5 is shown an example for foundation phase of an ARGE starting up from pre-contract. The Company AB GmbH forms a bidding consortium with company XY GbR.

---

93 Schwarz, K. (2007), page 636.
94 Burchardt, H.-P., Pfülb, W. (1998), page 93.
95 Leimböck, E.; Iding, A. (2005), page 127.
96 Ibid., page 127.
97 Jagenburg, I.; Schröder, C. U. (2008), page 57.
98 Ibid., page 57.
99 http://ted.europa.eu/udl?uri=TED:NOTICE:28746-2012:TEXT:DE:HTML&src=0, date: 27.01.2012.
100 http://www.business-services.fraport.de/content/fraport_ag_business-services/de/misc/binaer/bewerber-_bietergemeinschaftserklaerung/jcr:content.file/bewerberbietergemeinschaftserklaerung_pl.pdf, date: 08.02.2012.

As first step they set up a pre-contract which defines the framework for a later ARGE agreement. The ARGE arises only in case of contract with the principal.

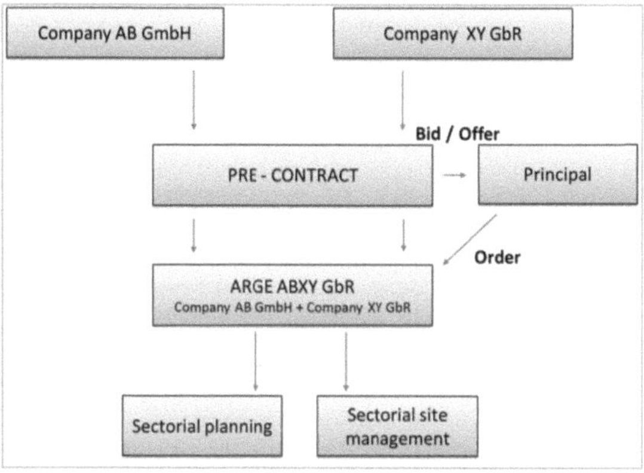

Figure 5: Transfer from pre-contract to ARGE agreement[101]

Pre-contract and the ARGE agreement have to be kept apart. BiGe ends with acquisition of the contract, and the ARGE starts with the acquisition. The pre-contract ends with subscription of the main contract[102]. So there are two separate partnerships[103]. The pre-contract contains not automatically the common purpose and the mutual encouragement to reach the goals. So in worst case it is possible that a BiGe partnership acquires a contract, but ARGE contract negotiations do not lead in a successful partnership. Reason therefore could be that partners do not achieve an agreement in share-ownership ratio. Partners are already several liable in relation to the principal, although they had not achieved an internal agreement. In general, principal has not to think about internal ARGE difficulties. When the project process is interrupted by the ARGE, the principal could claim compensation[104].

[101] Compiled by the author.
[102] Ulmer, C.; Schäfer, P. (2009) page 135.
[103] Burchardt, H.-P., Pfülb, W. (1998), page 1025.
[104] Burchardt, H.-P., Pfülb, W. (1998), page 1026.

In general the pre-contract is limited to the obligation that the parties are willing to enter into an ARGE agreement[105]. However it is useful to define necessary requirements for foundation of the ARGE in the pre-contract. For example should be defined in pre-contract the successful acquisition of the project or the common purpose of the partnership and the liability for contributions.

Partners are entitled to found the partnership according to section 894 of ZPO. The pre-contract can be terminated by when concerned partner propounds important reasons.

However a Partnership under Civil Law could also be founded by conclusive behaviour[106]. In this case the partners sometimes do not know that they are entered into a partnership. In general, when in construction industry only one partner appears externally, it will be assumed that there must be a subcontract. Pre-contracts are legally Partnerships under Civil Law[107].

In any case of dispute, must be apparent for justice the presumed will of the partners. In other case the pre-contract was ineffective[108]. Engineer contracts have to be divided in the description of the work and the price description[109].

In pre-contract and also later in the ARGE agreement, has to be defined a non-competition clause. The non-competition clause is coupled with the duty of loyalty. Due to duty of loyalty it is forbidden for the partners to take part with their companies in the same bidding procedure for a construction project as the ARGE. Every partner has to be careful, if there is a non-competition clause in the contract[110].

The ARGE should have a mutual bank account, invoices should be paid from this bank account and investment should be accomplished mutually. For example the rental of a construction side office.

As described, Partnerships under Civil Law are exempted from formalities. Considering their own interests, ARGE members should conclude an explicitly agreement[111]. That

---

105 Ulmer C.; Schäfer, P. (2009): ,page 135.
106 Lang, F. et al. (2010), page 44 .
107 Ibid., page 44.
108 Wirth, A. et al. (2004), page 47.
109 Häußermann, D. et al. (2008), page 35.
110 Jagenburg, I.; Schröder, C. U. (2008), page 149.
111 Lang, F. et al. (2010), page 44.

means that arrangements are committed deliberately and in full knowledge. The general form is in written form.

7 Internal relationship

7.1 Bodies and their tasks

Differing from section 705 et seq. of BGB, an ARGE has other bodies[112]. According to the model contract, there are the partners' meeting, technical management, commercial management and construction management. The model contract defines the partners' meeting as supreme body for questions of principle[113].

The partners' meeting is the highest institution within an ARGE[114]. In this context the partners' meeting is also called board of directors. Towards the common purpose, the board of directors in this case has not only the obligation of control, it has a double function[115]. The partners' meeting is also a decisions-making body; therefore the decisions must be implemented by management.

In the ARGE agreement has to be defined which decisions are necessary to be decided by the partners' meeting. So the partners' meeting has the responsibility to decide about questions, which are not in the range of authority of the management[116]. In general, fundamental questions like bank loans, changes in ARGE agreement or contract extension should be approved by the partners' meeting[117]. Frequency of meetings can be determined if necessary. ARGE model contract defines, that partners have to be invited to the partners' meetings in time.

Partners' meeting is an assembly for all partners. So all partners have to be invited, and neither of the partners could be excluded from the meeting[118]. Concerning the quorum could be defined each form of majority. Contrary to this regulation, in section 709 of BGB is the principle of unanimity defined. Indeed this form of majority lames the decision making authority of the partners' meeting. Useful is an agreement with qualified majority decisions.

---

[112] According to the ARGE model contract of German Construction Industry Federation and the Chamber of Architects in Baden-Württemberg.
[113] Jagenburg, I.; Schröder, C. U. (2008), page 1116.
[114] Burchardt, H.-P., Pfülb, W. (1998), page 175.
[115] Ibid., page 176.
[116] Messerschmidt, B.; Thierau, T. (2007a), page 21.
[117] Ibid., page 21.
[118] Model Contract Chamber of Architects (2005), page 9.

In practice engineering firms are interested in establishing a management board with high competencies. So that time-consuming and cumbersome meetings are not necessary in a high frequency.

According to the model contracts, technical and commercial management are divided. In contrast to section 709 and 714 of BGB follows the model contracts the way of oHG[119]. Reasons therefore are that the ARGE becomes slow and inefficient under one management resort. Main authority for decisions underlies commercial and technical management.

Technical and commercial management are executive organs of the partners' meeting[120]. The two management resorts could be perceived by one partner or occupied by two different partners. Main task of the two management bodies is the fulfilment of the contract for work and services. The division of the technical and management is not only a division of tasks and responsibilities; it is also a limitation and allocation of management authorities and representation of the respective resorts[121]. The commercial management expenses should not be underestimated. The commercial management is responsible for tax matters, accounting, orders and receiving invoices, etc.[122] In case of culpable conduct; management is liable towards his partners[123]. Project management could be also accomplished by the commercial management.

In the model contract for architects is described, that the technical and commercial management could be combined to one resort. In this case all responsibilities will be bundled in the hand of one partner or even one person. This could have the advantage that coordination between the management resorts is not more necessary, because of union in one resort. This could lead to flexible and quick decisions. Disadvantage could be that other partners had less influence in decisions.

The planning and site management could be divided into two bodies. Reasons therefore are that the site management starts later and the focus on services differ from each other. Two bodies are resorts with limited competence[124]. Planning and site management are executive bodies. The main tasks to fulfil the contract are accomplished by these two

---

[119] Jagenburg, I.; Schröder, C. U. (2008), page 151.
[120] Messerschmidt, B.; Thierau, T. (2007a), page 22.
[121] Jagenburg, I.; Schröder, C. U. (2008), page 152.
[122] Messerschmidt, B.; Thierau, T. (2007a), page 23.
[123] Ibid., page 23.
[124] Burchardt, H.-P., Pfülb, W. (1998), page 178.

bodies[125]. All bodies above are depending on these resorts. Although their competencies are limited, they accomplish in practice also the tasks of the technical and commercial management[126]. In figure 4 are shown the bodies of ARGE with their mutual relationships.

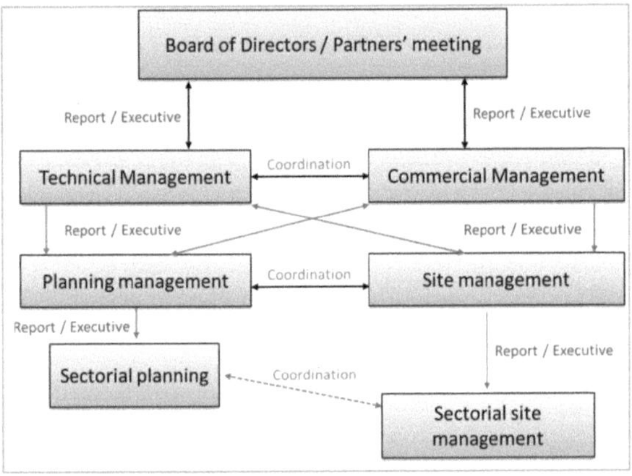

Figure 6: Bodies of ARGE[127]

Each resort has authority to give directives downwards. Otherwise each resort has to give a feedback and report to higher resorts. Commercial management has also the responsibility for bank account and all the payments and incomes. Resorts on one level have to coordinate each other. For example invoices which have to be paid by the commercial management have to be verified in coordination with the technical management. Services have to be accomplished before paying invoices.

Partners have to define in the agreement how to fill the head of departments. Legally, the partners are jointly entitled to manage the business of the partnership[128]. In construction industry it is important to achieve fast decisions, for this it is necessary to transfer authority.

Particularly important is the decision of which partner takes the chair of which department. Coming up with this question is the decision of transferring external

[125] Ibid., page 179.
[126] Ibid., page 179.
[127] According to Messerschmidt, B.; Thierau, T. (2007a), page 22 et. seq.
[128] BGB (2009), section 709.

representation to one of the partners. These regulations could be linked to different facts.

In case of a partnership with two partners, the management and the departments of planning and construction site management could be split balanced. One of the partners could take the head in technical management and the other partner could take the head in commercial management. With this allocation both partners could have external responsibility and authority to decide. Limitations of their competencies according to the restrictions of the management resort they are leading must be considered.

Another example to share the responsibilities and authorities for decisions is to couple the influence in management to the costs in construction each partner has to accomplish. This constellation is often applied in practice. However in practice there is a link to the fee which is defined in the contract to produce a work. The fee of engineers is calculated according to the HOAI on the basis of the construction costs in each trade. This division reflects the division by responsibility and liability in the ARGE. As later described, the limitation of liability could be also coupled to the engineering fee.

In the case of three or more partners it is possible respectively unavoidable, that one of the partners will not have influence in external decision-making and management responsibility. In this case it could be defined as mentioned before, that the partners allocate the head of management on the basis of engineering fee. ARGE partnerships with two partners could also apply this regulation.

Legally, a partner could not be excluded from management. Section 710 of BGB must be interpreted as abandonment for participation in management. Nevertheless, partners have the right for information and also a right for contradiction[129].

The expenditures and costs for managing the ARGE must be considered, but there must also be an eye on legal requirements. Nevertheless the ARGE has to accomplish one construction project and all bodies and structures of the ARGE must be trained to accomplish the project economically efficient. So there can be useful consolidations of resorts.

---

[129] Jagenburg, I.; Schröder, C. U. (2008), 156.

7.2 Contributions and performance

Obligation of the partners to support the purpose of the cooperation arises from the partnership agreement according to BGB section 705. According to their share in ARGE, partners have to fulfil their rights and obligations[130]. Obligations of the partners must be defined in the ARGE contract[131]. Liability to pay contributions is an important contractual task within the cooperation. For example, contributions could be payments, monetary goods like machines or the delegation of employees.

Payments of contributions have to be defined in the partnership agreement. If payments of contributions are not mentioned in the contract, prescribes the BGB in section 706, that the partners have to make equal contributions[132]. In this section it is also defined, that the contribution of partners could also consist in performance of services[133]. That means not necessarily that contributions have to be rendered in equal parts. As described before, contributions could be leaned on turnover or in the case of engineering firms on proportionately fee.

In ARGE commentaries there is a differentiation between services and contributions. For engineering firms is this differentiation not necessary. Reasons therefore are, that services in engineering are comparable with the planning procedure and contributions are employees and monetary. Contributions and performance can be treated equally in the contract[134]. Both are purpose benefiting instruments for the ARGE.

Obligation to perform and duty to render recoupment charges are limited by section 707 of BGB[135]. The amount and the time of contributions and services have to be defined in the partners meeting.

The designation of the purpose of the ARGE in the agreement, constitutes a limitation of the ARGE resources. Neither of the parties could be forced to use the resources for other purposes[136]. Another limitation of contribution and services results from the share

[130] Burchardt, H.-P., Pfülb, W. (1998), page 137.
[131] Jagenburg, I.; Schröder, C. U. (2008), page 118.
[132] BGB (2009), section 706.
[133] Ibid., section706.
[134] Burchardt, H.-P., Pfülb, W. (1998), page 149.
[135] Burchardt, H.-P., Pfülb, W. (1998), page 146.
[136] Ibid., page 147.

of the partners in the ARGE. This protects the partners against unduly utilisation and demands.

Partners have to concern their obligations: duty of allegiance, duty of encouragement, obligation to cooperate, duty to keep confidential, prohibition of competition, and contribution of services.

However there are also services, which have to be performed without limitation. For example administration of business could not be limited. Management duties have to be fulfilled according to requirements.

In common, the partners have to yield different services so that it is usual that one partner has to bring in more services and contributions than others. There are for example payroll accounting and supply of equipment[137]. Management of the ARGE is also labour intensive. In common the ARGE for engineering firms, has to work under the aegis of one partner.

In case of slightly additional work, ownership structure has not to be changed necessarily. For example the ARGE has a contract about planning and supervising technical systems within an administration building and gets a few months later an additional contract also to plan the outside facilities. This could cause, that the HVAC planner has to plan the drainage and the engineering firm for electrical systems has to plan the outdoor lighting installations. Considering the construction costs of the main contract, the additional contract is relatively small. So ownership-ratio could be the same.

Especially the provision of employees is very important in ARGE partnerships between engineering firms. The reason is that engineering firms are providing services which are accomplished by employees. The members shall deploy suitable and adequately qualified staff for providing the services under the contract[138]. So the ARGE members have a high responsibility for selecting the right employees for the right position. In ARGE agreement should be defined, how much employees at which time are at least necessary[139].

---

[137] Ibid., page 149.
[138] Burchardt, H.-P., Pfülb, W. (1998), page 454.
[139] Ibid., page 454.

There are different ways for employment of labour. First of all there is delegation. In this case the ARGE member transfers employment and instruction rights to the ARGE. However the employment contract between the ARGE member and the employee will be sustained.

The second form is exemption. In this case the employment contract between the ARGE member and the employee will be inactive. The employee has a direct relationship to the ARGE. Exempted employees have to be paid by the ARGE. The ARGE could also appoint new employees. In this case the ARGE has direct employee contracts with the employees. The ARGE members are not directly involved.

The main form to involve employees is the way of delegation. Employment payments are still assigned by the ARGE members. The ARGE members get there expenses back by profit distribution.

In the ARGE agreement should be defined, that each ARGE member is responsible for his part of the planning stage. Employees which are employed at subcontracting companies have not to be mentioned in the ARGE agreement.

Application of fund differs serious from the common regulations in BGB. According to law regulations[140], each partner is allowed to demand his proportion of the profit each year. In contrast in ARGE partnerships have to be defined other regulations. ARGE should pay out profit at the end of the project. There is a risk that partners have to carry out back payments.

[140] BGB (2009): section 721.

7.3 Contravention

In the ARGE agreement has to be regulated the case when one partner does not meet his obligations. To fulfil the contract to produce a work, it is necessary that all partners achieve the tasks for which they are responsible. Underperformance of one partner leads to increasing efforts for the other members considering the joint and several liabilities[141]. Therefore, sanctions must be defined and regulated in the ARGE agreement.

There are different possibilities to sanction the defaulting partner. For example there could be defined a reduction of the share in the ARGE. For worst cases could be also defined the exclusion of a partner. Partner could be in arrears with his contributions and performances. Examples therefore are delayed submission of the final design planning or understaffed construction management. Management of ARGE has to fix a written deadline, to admonish the defaulting partner. If the partner does not fulfil his service until the deadline, he is in arrears and has to reckon with contractual penalties. Generally, in the partnership agreement could be defined stricter regulations than in BGB.

Starting from the premise that the partner is not willing to render his service over an extended period of time, he has to be faced with contractual penalties. Contractual penalties could be started from penalty payments over change in ownership-ratio to excluding the partner.

Engineering firms have to consider, excluding a partner, they still have to fulfil the contract with the principal. So they need another partner to render all necessary services. But it is also not easy to integrate a new member in the ARGE. The new member of the ARGE is also liable for former businesses of the ARGE[142]. In practice the new firm will not enter the ARGE because of liability for services and transaction which has been accomplished by other firms. In practice the new partner wants to be subcontracted.

[141] Bärwaldt, R. (2002), page 1102.
[142] Jagenburg, I.; Schröder, C. U. (2008), page 347.

Arrears partner are not prevented against compensations for consequential losses by payments for contractual penalties[143]. Contractual penalty payments could be taken into account with compensations for consequential losses. Also unaffected is the contractual claim to fulfil the remaining.

According to section 723 of BGB the partner could be excluded when he is acting grossly negligent or intentional. A general example for wrongdoing could be non-performance in provision of fund or security bonds. An example in engineering firms for non-performance concerning delivery dates, is for example the delayed handing in of a draft planning or in not filling the position of supervisor.

On the other side, partners have also to right for exclusion of performance. One case in law for excluding the performance: When it is impossible for the obligor or for any body other person to accomplish the performance[144].

Contradiction of a partner could lead to irreconcilable differences within the partnership. So it is important to decide from case to case which sanctions are helpful and which are not. The ARGE partners have also to consider their responsibility and liability against the principal. They have to rebuke partners to secure themselves.

[143] BGB (2009), section 340.
[144] Ibid., section 275.

7.4 Internal Liability

Internal liability regards liability between the ARGE members. In this context, liability towards the principal remains unaffected. What applies here as well, if nothing otherwise is agreed in ARGE contract, the partners are liable according to section 708 of BGB. In this law is described that ARGE partners are liable for grossly negligent acting of each other. However there are no insurance companies, which secure in dependence to this law[145]. Reasons therefore are that the law leaves a margin open. The law says "a partner is only liable, in discharging the duties incumbent upon him, for the care he customarily exercises in his own affairs"[146]. This occurs, that subjective interpretations of grossly negligent acting are allowed.

For this reason the ARGE model contracts exclude liability in accordance to section 708 of BGB and define instead of it the liability in accordance to section 276 of BGB. According to this section of law, misconduct acting of partners could be determined objective. Here is defined that each form of intent and negligence is liable.

For internal relationships can be agreed a so called liability privilege. Liability privilege means that the ARGE members are only liable for gross negligence, not for slight negligence[147]. Gross negligence occurs when due diligence is being violated in a particular way.

According to section 722 of BGB, each partner has the same share on liabilities if the ARGE agreement nothing otherwise defines. When the ARGE agreement defines only a share on profit, than automatically the share on losses underlies the same participation[148] same share according to section 722 BGB. Thus the partners want another share than division per partners, they have to define it in the ARGE agreement.

Regardless of joint liability in relation to the principal has to be defined in the ARGE agreement, that each partner is responsible and liable for his own services. So in the ARGE agreement for engineering companies has to be defined, that each partner is liable for his own trade services, he has to accomplish. Each partner is responsible for the management tasks he is the head of.

---

145 Müller, M. (2012): Interview.
146 BGB (2009), Section 708.
147 Burchardt, H.-P., Pfülb, W. (1998), page 117.
148 BGB (2009), section 722.

7.5 Withdrawal or exclusion of an ARGE member

As described in the previous chapter, there are different reasons for excluding a partner. As mentioned it could be the last contravention step in contractual dispute with a partner. However the partner has also the right to leave the ARGE when there are valid reasons[149]. Termination of an ARGE cannot be easily assessed. Payment difficulties, incapability to fulfil the contractual obligations for secondment of personnel and even economic collapse of the partner are not valid reasons for an exit out of the ARGE[150].

In practice remaining ARGE partners have to decide from case to case. A partner who is not more willing to stay in ARGE could harm the partnership. It could be better for them to disband the non-performing partner, before he is harming the other partners due to jointly and several liabilities. In any case of withdrawal or exclusion has the principal no legal entitlement for information[151]. With the withdrawal of a partner does the ARGE not lose his identity.

When a partner leaves, he is still liable for the ARGE. His liability continues after the date of his exit for five years[152]. The leaving partner has to be participated on profit and loss until the moment of leaving. The consequence of retirement of an ARGE partner differs completely from retirement of a partner according to section 738 et seq. of BGB[153]. The ARGE remains in force. The remaining partners gain the participation of the leaven partner by accretion.

The ARGE could be also confronted with the insolvency of one of the members. In section 728 of BGB is defined, that the partnership has to be dissolved after insolvency of one of the ARGE members. In both model contracts is defined, that the ARGE continuous in any case of exclusion of one of the partners[154]. With the opening of insolvency proceedings the ARGE member will be automatically excluded from the ARGE.

---

[149] BGB (2009), section 723.
[150] Burchardt, H.-P., Pfülb, W. (1998), page 761.
[151] Burchardt, H.-P., Pfülb, W. (1998), page 755.
[152] Lang, V. (2000), page 122.
[153] Bärwaldt, R. (2002), page 1133.
[154] According to the ARGE model contract of German Construction Industry Federation section 24 and the Chamber of Architects in Baden-Württemberg section 12.

To preserve the ARGE from claims for damages from principal's side, should the ARGE be continued. The other ARGE members have to continue the ARGE with new partition. The share of the leaving partner has to be divided to the remaining partners. The remaining partners have still to fulfil the contract to produce a work with the principal. When the remaining partners could accomplish the residual works, they could finish the work without bringing a new partner in the ARGE. In this case, the principal has also not the legal entitlement or the authority to decide, if the new partner could participate in the ARGE[155].

In the model contracts is also defined, that in case of a two partners ARGE the remaining partner has also the obligation to continue the ARGE. There are legal objections and discussions if the partnerships could be continued by only one member[156]. However in context of this essay could not treated in detail. Fact is that the partner has to fulfil the contract and continue accomplishment.

When the ARGE partners could not complete the work with their portfolio of services, they are constrained to integrate or involve a new partner. In this context must be considered, that a new partner is also liable for inherited liability[157]. In the ARGE agreement could this regulation excluded, but in practice it is difficult to differ between damages and losses, and consequential losses which could be arisen from an earlier event.

If the leaving company has management responsibilities must these transferred to the remaining partners. The partners have to decide in the partners' meeting about fulfilment of the resorts.

In figure 7 is shown an example from legal practice. There is visualized the case of an insolvency partner in a partnership of three.

---

155 Burchardt, H.-P., Pfülb, W. (1998), page 755.

156 http://www.brennecke-partner.de/110164/Das-Recht-der-GbR-Teil-5-1-Wechsel-der-Gesellschafter, date 07.02.2012.

157 BGH (2003): Judgement from 07.04.2003 – II ZR 56/02, in NJW 2003, 1803.

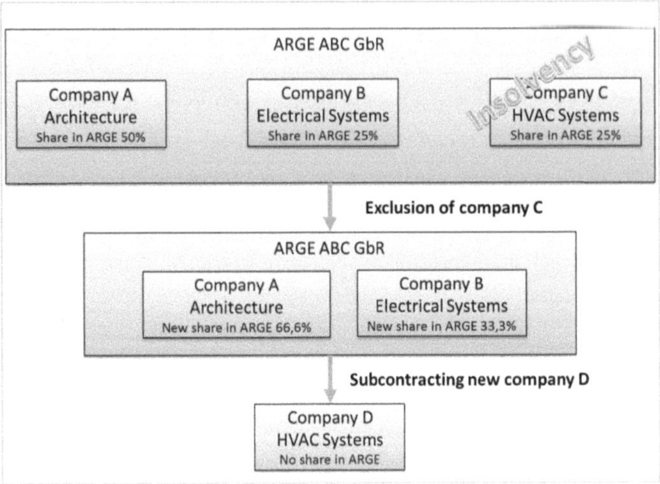

Figure 7: Example for insolvency of an ARGE partner[158]

Three planning firms, in this case an architecture office, an engineering firm for electrical systems and an engineering firm for HVAC – systems decide to found an ARGE for accomplishing of a construction project. During the construction process one of the partners – company C gets insolvent. The principal has signed a contract with the company "ARGE ABC GbR". So he is willing to get the defined purpose from this ARGE. The ownership-share of the remaining two partners will increase according to their share ratio.

In this example the leaving engineering firm opens a gap in service portfolio of the ARGE. None of the remaining partner could fill the lack in service. So they need a new partner. According to this example from practice is the new engineering firm not interested in entering the ARGE. They engineering firm would not participate in jointly and several liability. Thus the ARGE has to subcontract the engineering firm for HVAC – systems. This company will not have share in ARGE and therefore no influence in decisions within the ARGE. The ARGE is the principal for the new engineering firm.

ARGE partners could prepare the ARGE to absorb difficulties which come up with the difficulties of insolvency of a partner. One possibility could be contract surety bonds.

[158] Compiled by the author.

With the exclusion of the insolvency partner the ARGE has to set up a dissolution balance sheet[159]. On one side the dissolution balance sheet could help the remaining ARGE partners to show up payable accounts of the departed partner and on the other side the balance sheet could help the excluded partner to claim demands for profit that accrued during the term of ARGE partnership[160].

[159] Burchardt, H.-P., Pfülb, W. (1998), page 793.
[160] Ibid., page 793.

7.6 Performance bond

First of all, the performance bond is a contract between three parties: the creditor - for example the bank, the engineering firm as debtor and the principal as beneficiary. Principal could expect from ARGE a guarantee to fulfil the contract[161].

In figure 8 is visualized the relationship between the three bond parties. In this picture is shown an example for performance bond.

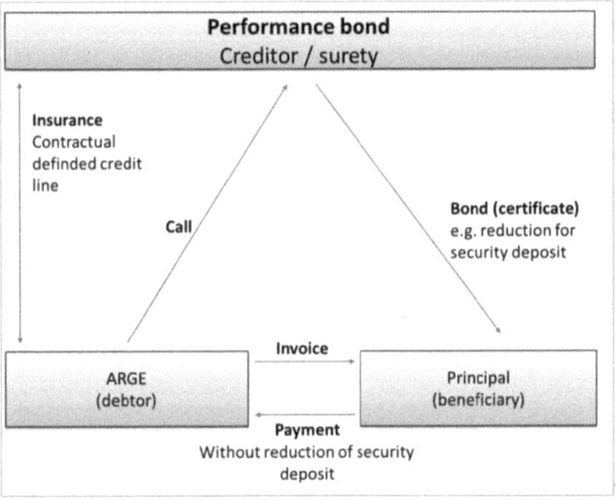

Figure 8: Performance bond relationship[162]

The principal demands as part of signing the contract to produce a work a contract surety bond. So the ARGE calls a debtor, in general a bank or an insurance company.

Important in this context is also the possibility for the other ARGE members to protect themselves against insolvency of one member. Krause – Allenstein points out, that partners could be protected against insolvency of one ARGE members by closing

[161] Burchardt, H.-P., Pfülb, W. (1998), page 661.
[162] According to http://www.buergschaft24.de/tl_files/BB24/Vertragsbeziehungen-in-der-kautionsversicherung.jpg, date: 28.01.2012.

individual performance bonds[163]. This performance bond secures the range of service of the partner. Considered must be the condition that the performance bond has to be issued directly to the principal.

After occurrence of the insolvency and the linkage to closing the ARGE, have the remaining partners to wait, until the insolvency administrator rejects the fulfilment of the contract. After rejection occurs the guarantee case. After contract fulfilment by remaining ARGE partners goes the claim of principal over to the remaining partners according to section 426 of BGB.

The better way to reduce internal liability is the usage of so called back bonds[164]. The back bond model is a double stage bond model: Due to demand of principal, has the ARGE to bring up a performance bond. To enable hand out of the performance bond, the ARGE partners have to bring up a performance bond in relation to the ARGE[165].

Each partner has to close a performance bond for his services towards the ARGE. These bonds will be used as bundled performance bonds between ARGE and principal. When ARGE will be claimed by the principal, the ARGE has to set up claims against his partners. When ARGE was not claimed, the partnership could also not come up with claims against his partners. Disadvantage of this model are the higher costs.

[163] Krause-Allenstein, F. (2007), page 624.
[164] Burchardt, H.-P., Pfülb, W. (1998), page 661.
[165] Ibid., page 661.

8 External relationship

8.1 External representation

According to BGB section 709, the partners are jointly entitled to manage the business of the partnership. For each transaction the approval of all partners is required[166]. The principle of general management with the requirement of unanimity can be advantageous for each partner. All decisions must be verified by each partner[167]. However this handling is impractical und cumbersome. Partners have to find for each decision a majority or even absolute majority.

According to BGB section 711 can be also defined, that each partner is allowed to manage the business. In this case must be defined in the partnership agreement: Each manager is individually authorised for management and representation[168]. In this case authorities are not bundled to one person. This situation could also be infeasible.

In the partnership agreement can be defined other regulations. For example there can be the definition that the majority of votes decide. So there is also necessity for practical handling of the ARGE management. The ARGE model contracts point out other regulations.

In this case, the other partners have the right of objection. But this right cannot be applied in an arbitrary manner. The partners have to focus the interests of the ARGE.

It is usual to divide the tasks according to the performance of the partners, thus the responsibility of the partners have also to be confined[169]. According to the model contract of German Construction Industry Federation, the management is divided in technical management and commercial management. This definition could be adapted to an ARGE contract with engineering firms.

Technical and commercial tasks differ from each other fundamentally. Both tasks are labour intensive, so that the division of these two resorts could be useful. Depending on the size of the project and the contract with the principal could be practical to involve a

[166] BGB (2009), section 709.
[167] Lang, V. (2000), page 91.
[168] Ibid., page 92.
[169] Lang, V. (2000), page 93.

company which is specialized in project management. This firm could be responsible for commercial management and the other engineering firms could focus their resources on the planning and construction management tasks.

Both management bodies are able to represent the ARGE outward. Each of them is in the position to sign contracts as long as the responsibilities are defined in the ARGE agreement or they are assigned by the partners' meeting to act. It must be also considered, which bodies of ARGE could be visible outward.

Considering liability of construction site manager, he has to be careful in relation to the contract with the principal. Responsibilities of site management have to be clarified with the principal. For example could come up difficulties in countersigning daily wages of the executive companies.

8.2 Liability

Limitation of liability in relation to the principal is unusual. The principal must agree. The principal will not have any interest in circumcision of ARGE liability[170]. The internal liability could be limited in the ARGE agreement. The type of Dach – ARGE allows a differentiation of services which have to be provided by the partners.

According to the adjudication of the BGH, has the GbR legal capacity and has the capacity to sue and be sued[171]. Architects and Engineers have other obligations of liability than the building contractor. Architects and Engineers are responsible for development and planning of buildings free from defects; the contractor is responsible for building free from defects[172]. As described, the partners of an ARGE are jointly and severally liable[173]. This affects also warranty claims of the principal; regardless of the internal contractual relationships of the ARGE partners[174].

The contractor has to provide the principal with work which is free of material defects at the time of acceptance. The work is free of material defects at the time of acceptance if it is in the agreed condition and complies with generally accepted engineering practice[175]. If the condition has not been agreed, the work is free of material defects at the time of acceptance, when it is suitable for the use presupposed by the contract, otherwise is suitable for customary use and is in a condition which is usual for structures of the same type and which the principal can expect in line with the type of work.

So acceptance has major importance for the contractor. The acceptance represents the start of the warranty period for all parts of which the acceptance relates and which have been accepted without defect. Furthermore the acceptance declaration reverses the burden of explanation and proof for the contractual performance of work insofar as the work is accepted free of defects. Until the time of acceptance, the contractor bears the burden of explanation and proof for the fact that he has performed his work in compliance with the contract. This burden of explanation and proof passes to the

[170] Bärwaldt, R. (2002), page 1130.
[171] BGH (2001): Judgement from 29.01.2001 – II ZR 331/00, in NJW 2001, 1056.
[172] Wirth, A. et al. (2004), page 49.
[173] Bärwaldt, R. (2002), page 1102.
[174] Ibid., page 1130.
[175] Mütze, M. et al. (2007), page 172.

principal at the time of acceptance. This does not apply to those parts of the work which the principal reported as being defective at the time of acceptance – so called acceptance defects. The contractor must perform this work in compliance with the contract as remaining work still to be completed and explain and prove its compliance with the contract[176].

One consequence of the contractor owing success is in particular that, regardless of blame, he has to remedy any defects in the work which occur during performance of the construction work or the warranty period[177]. In figure 9 is shown the schematic transfer of liability.

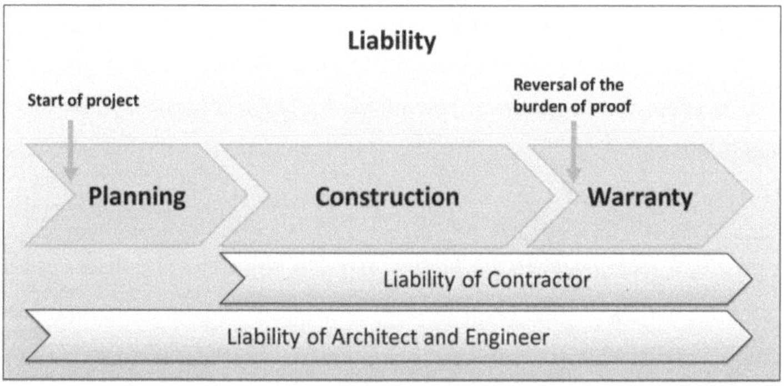

Figure 9: Liability for construction project[178]

Architects and Engineers are responsible from the beginning of the project. As specialist they have the duty to advise the principle. Starting the construction of the project, the liability of the contractor starts.

As shown in picture 9, in construction phase are not only executing companies liable. Architects and Engineers are also liable for their planning and site management.

Generally the planners have not only to plan the building; they have also to accomplish the site management on behalf of the builder. Disputes between principals and architects

[176] Mütze, M. et al. (2007), page 170.
[177] VOB/B section 13.
[178] Compiled by the author.

or engineers are often complicated. For example, when electrical installations in the building are not free of defects, has the principals the mentioned rights according to BGB, as long as the contract defines nothing else. When it becomes obvious that the firm for electrical systems had installed according to agreements with the sectorial site management, than the engineering firm could be also confronted with warranty claims. This case is simplified, and there are such more legal and contractual relationships, which could prevent or reduce warranty claims against the planners. However this scenario is not beside the point. In practice will the principal try to enforce warranty claims – if needed against all involved parties.

Due to the planning process, architects and engineers have to hand in different steps in planning. For example there are the Final Design Planning or the Implementation Planning[179]. After handing in the plans the principal has to proof the plans and to release the payments according to HOAI. Each of this approvals by the principal illustrate a form of exemptions for the planners. The principal accepts the plans in form and quality at this point of time.

As described an important milestone in construction projects is the reversal of the burden of proof. Here changes the burden of proof from the contractor, architect or engineer to the principal. The reversal of the burden of proof will be carried out by acceptance[180]. Before this moment the planner has to burden, that his services are free from defects. After this moment the principal has to attest the building does not fulfil the contract requirements[181].

When the performed work and services are defective, than the principal has the opportunity for warranty claims. According to section 634 of BGB is the time for warranty claims limited to five years, starting with acceptance. In BGB are defined different methods for enforcement of warranty claims.

First of all there is the right of the principal to demand cure[182]. The principal has also the right to remedy the defect himself and demand reimbursement for required expenses[183]. If the defect could be repaired the principal has also the right to reduce

[179] Mütze, M. et al. (2007), page 141.
[180] Boldt, A. (2005), page 123.
[181] BGB (2009), section 640.
[182] Ibid., section 635.
[183] Ibid., (2009), section 637.

payment[184]. Furthermore the principal could demand compensation or demand reimbursement of futile expenditure[185].

The warranty period is one of the reasons, why the ARGE does not end with accomplishing the construction of the building. Disbandment of ARGE could start with payment of the final invoice.

In certain cases the acceptance of the work is not possible, due to the character of the work. For these cases, there is a special provision in section 646 of BGB. In place of acceptance there is an accomplishment of the work. Examples for this works are concerts, transport industry or theatrical performance. Architecture and engineering contracts cannot be accepted by completion of the construction project. In architecture and engineering contracts is a declared acceptance unusual[186].

So in most cases the acceptance of the work will be accomplished by approving the work. Approval can be accomplished by reception of the constructions plans and documents. Acceptance could also be accomplished by a coherent way, for example by payment of the fee invoice or by using or utilizing the constructed building[187].

So the consequences for the ARGE are: management has to be careful in bringing services to account and get the payment. Management has to aware of importance of accomplishing planning steps and linkage to payment.

184 Ibid., (2009), section 638.
185 Ibid., (2009), section 284 and 638.
186 Wirth, A. et al. (2004), page 115.
187 Ibid., page 115.

8.3 Insurance for external relationships

The German Insurance Association has developed special contractual conditions, which are defined in the model terms and conditions used by the insurance companies (BBR)[188]. BBR are model terms and conditions used by insurance companies. In this conditions are regulated, that the insurance company covers the engineering firm in specific cases. In BBR are also the ARGE partnerships regulated.

The scope of insurance cover is regulated in the ARGE clause of BBR. Important for insurance cover is, that the partner provides his freelance work legally and economically self-dependent.

In section 3.1 of BBR is regulated, that insurance cover consist to the insured sum. Requirement therefore is that tasks or construction phases within the ARGE are divided between the partners[189].

For the case that the tasks are not divided, the insurance cover will be reduced to the amount of holding, which is leaned on share of partners in the ARGE. If this quote-based calculation cannot be applied, than the calculation will be applied by the number of ARGE partners[190].

Depending on the share in the ARGE, there can be a huge difference in liability insurance coverage[191]. According to section 3.3 of BBR, are claims among each other not included. The insurance company want to protect himself against arrangements among the ARGE partners.

[188] Model terms and conditions for professional liability insurance of architects and engineers (2007), section A.
[189] Garbes, M. (2008), page 61.
[190] Ibid., page 61.
[191] Ibid., page 61.

8.4 Insolvency of ARGE

The ARGE is eligible for insolvency[192]. Partnership will be drained by opening the insolvency proceedings. According to section 15 of InsO, each partner of the ARGE is entitled to request the opening of insolvency proceeding[193]. Reasons for insolvency could be inability to pay or excessive indebtedness. Though excessive indebtedness could only occur in corporate enterprises[194].

Insolvency debtor is the ARGE, not the ARGE partners[195]. The ARGE partners have the duty to cooperate and duty of disclosure according to section 101 of InsO. Administrative authority and power of disposal will be transferred to the insolvency administrator[196].

Assets in the insolvency are the assets of the company and the social entitlements of the ARGE partners. Furthermore there are claims against the ARGE partners. For example there are claim for damages due to breach of duty to care and breach of duty of allegiance[197]. Depending on the ARGE agreement there could be also demands on outstanding debts and services.

Consequently, ARGE partner could be insolvency creditor or preferential creditor. As insolvency creditor the partner has claims against the ARGE, for example in form of unpaid invoices. As preferential creditor the partner has objects he has cede to the ARGE.

Liability of partners could be accomplished according to section 128 of HGB. There is defined, that partner are jointly and several liable for liabilities of the partnership. Finally the ARGE partners are jointly unlimited liable for the liabilities of the ARGE.

With acceptance of the insolvency administrator, ARGE could be continued. Opening the insolvency proceeding, leads to closing of the ARGE[198]. Opening the insolvency

---

192 http://www.uni-marburg.de/fb01/studium/zusatzqualifikation/privates_baurecht/vorlesunge /baurecht_materialien/ws0607_materialien/baurecht_messerschmidt/ws0607_baurecht_arge0, date: 08.02.2012.

193 InsO (2011), section 15.

194 Burchardt, H.-P., Pfülb, W. (1998), page 772.

195 Lang, F. et al. (2010), page 338.

196 Ibid., page 338.

197 Ibid., page 338.

198 http://www.uni-marburg.de/fb01/studium/zusatzqualifikation/privates_baurecht/vorlesunge

proceedings could be defeated due to lack of assets. This circumstances leads not to insolvency proceedings and closing of the ARGE according to section 728 of BGB. Delayed filling of insolvency could be valued as criminal act in Germany.

/baurecht_materialien/ws0607_materialien/baurecht_messerschmidt/ws0607_baurecht_arge0, date: 08.02.2012.

9 Closing and disorganization of the ARGE

There are different reasons for completion the ARGE. Basically must be differed between closing the ARGE due to fulfilment of purpose[199] and closing the ARGE due to termination. Closing an ARGE could only be accomplished by involving the principal, with the exception of insolvency. In picture 10 are shown the external relationships and dependencies from the principal to close an ARGE.

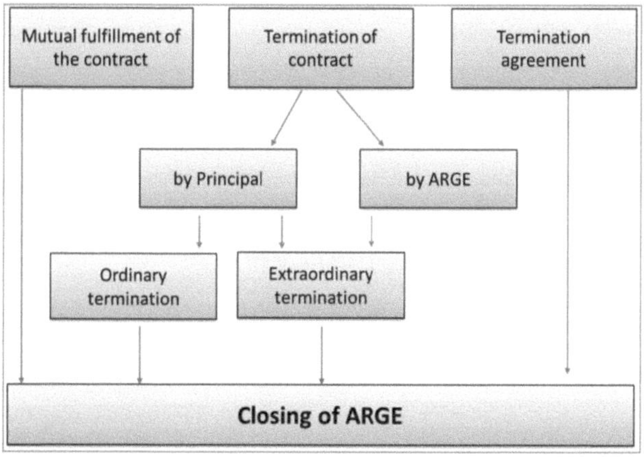

Figure 10: Ways of contractual exit[200]

As pictured in figure 10, the regular way to finish the partnership is coupled with the achievement of the objectives[201]. It must be considered, that the fulfilment is not reached with the end of the construction works on the site.

To close the ARGE, the partnership has to fulfil all responsibilities. Included are also all warranty deeds. All legal relationships have to wind up. With the achievement of the objectives starts the closing process.

[199] BGB (2009), section 726
[200] According to Wirth, A. et al (2004), page 98
[201] Bärwaldt, R. (2002), page 1131

As well possible is the way over a termination agreement. In this case the principal and the ARGE arrange a contractual agreement for terminating the contract. This case is not unusual in practice. For example could it be that the principal wants to build up a new production facility and during the planning process with the ARGE, an economic crisis comes up and the principal has to stop investments. The ARGE partners would not insist on contract fulfilment, considering further orders by the principal.

In German law has the ARGE not the possibility for ordinary termination. The principal should not reasonably expect and confronted with termination by the contractor[202]. Reasons therefore are that the principal would have to handle financial and time spending extraordinary charges.

However, the ARGE has the possibility of extraordinary termination of the contract. For example the ARGE could circumstantiate that the principal has not fulfilled his duty for cooperation and participation in planning and building process[203]. Another reason could be that the principal has not paid fulfilled services. Disruption in relationship between principal and ARGE is also a legally valid reason[204].

The principal has the right for extraordinary termination of the contract. In this case the principal has only to pay the accomplished services[205]. Termination by the principal is also complicated, but jurisdiction has documented in judgements that there are valid reasons for the principal to terminate the contract. Examples for valid reasons: lack in capability of permission, exceeding the costs, corruptly acting by the ARGE, lack of willingness to reengineer the planning due to self-caused bad planning.

In the assessment of the question, if there is a reason for an extraordinary termination, must be considered the mutual contractual duty for cooperation[206]. This applies for each contractual partner, who is motivated for extraordinary termination.

After the arrangement with the principal the closing of the ARGE could start. The disorganization and closing process in the ARGE is not detailed described in the model contracts. However it is not necessary to define other regulations than the BGB specifies.

---

[202] Wirth, A. et al. (2004), page 100
[203] BGB (2009), section 643
[204] Wirth, A. et al. (2004), page 105
[205] Ibid., page 104
[206] Wirth, A. et al. (2004), page 105.

Closing of partnership needs a period of time. First of all, with closing the ARGE changes the purpose of the ARGE. The acquiring partnership changes to a liquidation partnership[207].

The character of ARGE does not change, but the duties of the partners changes. The partners are obliged to enable the closing of the ARGE[208]. With the fulfilment of all responsibilities, for example accomplishing the warranty time with acceptance of the installations starts the closing procedure of the ARGE.

Dissolution of the ARGE is described in section 731 et seq. of BGB. In law, is regulated as first step, that the ARGE has to hand back the equipment of the partners. Here is mentioned equipment which the partners have left for us in the ARGE. Equipment which is necessary in accomplishing the closing the process has to stay in ARGE

Example therefore is the location of the ARGE. As mentioned should the ARGE addressed in the office of the ARGE management. Reasons therefore are that costs for running the ARGE can be reduced and handled. Therefore is an unavoidable mix of using the equipment between the ARGE and the partner's office. As mentioned, this equipment has to be used by the ARGE for accomplishing the closing process.

Terminating the ARGE is regulated in section 723 to 728 of BGB. Partners have to be careful about warranty and liability which can continue over years. For this reason the partners have to arrange additional conditions in the ARGE contract. The ARGE ends finally with completion with the end of warranty deed[209]. After the payment respectively acceptance of the closing invoice, the ARGE has to complete the balance sheet.

In the ARGE model contract is defined, that first of all the partners get their reimbursement of expenses. On the second step, the operating expenses will be covered[210]. Thereof concerned are not only debts with third parties, there are also demands of partners against the ARGE[211]. As third step will be paid back the bank

---

[207] Jagenburg, I.; Schröder, C. U. (2008), page 334.
[208] Ibid., page 334.
[209] Bärwaldt, R. (2002), page 1131.
[210] BGB (2009), section 733.
[211] Jagenburg, I.; Schröder, C. U. (2008), page 351.

loans. As fourth step provision is made for monthly adaption of member's accounts. And finally as fifth step is intended the pay-out according to share in partnership[212].

Due to the provisionally shifting liquidity to the members, it is allowed for the ARGE to secure the repayment claim[213]. Otherwise in case of insolvency after pay-out the other members have to compensate the deficit. Partners also protect themselves against other members facing non-performance.

---

212 Ibid., page 351.
213 Ibid., page 351.

10 Partial invalidity of ARGE

A partnership, based on a faulty or defeasible ARGE agreement is also called invalid ARGE. Reasons for an invalid ARGE can be, that the complete ARGE agreement, or terms of agreement are nullified[214].

Main reasons for reflection of the defective partnership are that there are difficulties in reversal of the contract, due to longevity ARGE with a lot of corresponding's and business with third parties.

First of all must be differentiated if the ARGE agreement was from the first incomplete. It must be determined if there was a lack of will for realization of the partnership purpose. When there was a lack, the partnership is not an invalid ARGE - the ARGE agreement was faulty from scratch[215].

The invalid ARGE implies that there was the will for realization of a partnership purpose[216]. Incorrect partnerships were common in corporate enterprises. The model of incorrect partnership agreements assumes that the partnership was not existent, when the partners had known before that their agreement is invalid. They would not transfer management and responsibility to another partner.

A severability clause has to be defined in ARGE agreements. This clause secures, that invalidity of several sections of the agreement do not lead to invalidity of the whole agreement[217]. In general the partners have the demand to continue the ARGE.

In this context must be recognized, that in an ARGE agreement could only be handled the partial invalidity. The complete invalidity could not be handled in a contract. It is also useful to couple the partners' obligation also to healing of partial invalidity[218].

According to section 139 and 140 of BGB there are healing possibilities. In this case the invalidity of ARGE could be overcome[219]. For example could be, that a partner continues his work, while he knows the faults in ARGE agreement. Consequently this

---

[214] Jagenburg, I.; Schröder, C. U. (2008), page 53.
[215] Ibid., page 57.
[216] Ibid., page 57.
[217] Burchardt, H.-P., Pfülb, W. (1998), page 957.
[218] Burchardt, H.-P., Pfülb, W. (1998), page 971.
[219] Jagenburg, I.; Schröder, C. U. (2008), page 58.

partner confirms the ARGE according section 141 and 144 of BGB. However there is not an obligation to heal the faulty agreement.

Contractual gaps do not lead to invalidity of the agreement[220]. Gaps have to be closed under stipulation of the will of partners and considering good faith and common usage[221].

[220] Ibid., page 375.
[221] BGB (2009): section 133 and 157.

11 Tax treatment of the ARGE

Preconditioned ARGE has the legal form of Partnership under Civil Law, taxation like a partnership according to section 15 of EStG[222] has to be accomplished. Internal partnerships like BeGe and inward turned Partnerships under Civil Law are not concerned. Therefore the ARGE itself has not to pay income tax or corporation tax.

The profit of the ARGE has to be determined uniformly and separately[223]. Share of profit has to be accomplished according to the arrangement of the ARGE agreement. ARGE partners with legal form of partnership have to add the profit from ARGE to their own income. This income has to be deducted with the income tax. ARGE partners with legal entity have to add the profit to their corporate income. Afterwards income has to be reduced by the corporation tax[224].

According to section 180 of the German Fiscal Code, the ARGE members are fiscal independent. They have not to accomplish a consistent and separate income determination – as long as purpose of the ARGE is focused on accomplishing one contract to produce a work[225]. The same belongs to the Trade Tax. According to section 2a of German Trade Tax Act, the ARGE is not a commercial enterprise, as long as the ARGE was founded to accomplish one project. The business premises of the ARGE are considered to be premises of the partners[226].

It must be considered, that the ARGE has to pay Trade Tax, when one of the partners is a corporation like a Limited Liability Company (GmbH). Here applies the infection theory: when one of the members is infected, all other partners will be affected[227].

The ARGE is subject to turnover tax[228]. As legally independent enterprise, the ARGE has to pay turnover taxes - independent from legal form. On the one hand underlie the payments which the ARGE reaches from the principal to turnover tax, and on the other

---

[222] Bärwaldt, R. (2002), page 1135.
[223] http://www.steuernetz.de/aav_steuernetz/lexikon/K-10646.xhtml?currentModule=home, date: 06.02.2012.
[224] http://www.hk24.de/recht_und_fair_play/steuerrecht/steuerexi_ordner/366794/Gesellschaft_buergerlichen_Rechts_Gruendung_und_Steuern.html;jsessionid=B4B748D72311FA80E7809B4C0F65425.repl21#10, date: 06.02.2012.
[225] Bärwaldt, R. (2002), page 1136.
[226] http://www.gesetze-im-internet.de/gewstg/__2a.html, date: 04.01.2012.
[227] Kieß, D. (2012), Interview.
[228] Burchardt, H.-P., Pfülb, W. (1998), page 617.

hand trade payables and related accounts, are liable to turnover tax. So the turnover tax is an item in transit. Internal partnership is not recognized from the point of view of turnover tax[229].

According to German Tax Law, the ARGE has the legal obligation to keep records[230]. Obligation starts with turnover per year of the ARGE at 500.000 EUR and a profit per year of 50.000 EUR[231].On behalf of the partners should be prepared a balance sheet and a profit and loss account. These documents could be basis for allocation of profits or additional payment liability. An ARGE is an independent partnership; it could not assessed as subsidiary of one of the partners[232].

For the employees, which are directly employed in the ARGE, must be withhold the income tax and paid to the local tax office. For delegated employees, are the partners responsible for the tax affairs of their employees[233]. In this context it is important to recognize, that the tax office is authorized to collect the whole outstanding tax claims from each of the joint and several debtors[234].

However the tax office has to apply according to law end equity[235]. Contributions of partners to the ARGE are not taxable[236]. The contributions of partners are compensated by profit and loss participation.

Moment of payment of performance and coupled tax payment steps in when the definition in contract to produce a work accomplishes. Due to long construction periods it is unpractical to get the payment at the end of the project. So in the contract to produce a work between the principal and the ARGE has to be defined, that advance payments are allowed and requested. In most cases the principal has also an interest in part payment. Input tax deductions are allowed. Accounting of ARGE treats the turnover tax as transit item. That means that the income tax neither has influence on construction expenditures nor increases the profit.

---

229 Ibid, page 618.
230 Ibid., Interview.
231 http://www.hk24.de/recht_und_fair_play/steuerrecht/steuerexi_ordner/366794/Gesellschaft_buergerlichen_Rechts_Gruendung_und_Steuern.html;jsessionid=B4B748D723111FA80E7809B4C0F65425.repl21#10, date: 06.02.2012.
232 Ibid, page 611.
233 Ibid., page 613.
234 Ibid., page 613.
235 Burchardt, H.-P., Pfülb, W. (1998), page 617.
236 Ibid., page 617.

From the legal point of view, the particularity of the ARGE consist in the fact that – unless agreed as contributions, which are "internal" and therefore no subject to value added tax – the supply of means or services according to §4.1 is based on bilateral contractual agreements, i.e. the means or services are supplied to the ARGE by the Partners as so-called "third-party". These "external" contractual relationships are subject to value added tax and i.e. consist of separate purchasing contracts for material, rental contracts for equipment and contracts regarding personnel, which are performed in addition to other contractual obligations, according to the terms and conditions agreed upon in this ARGE Agreement – including the restriction regarding slight negligence according to the Preface[237].

---

[237] Model Contract of German Construction Industry Federation (2005), section 4.

12 Conclusion

Recording is rewarding[238] - is a widely recognized German proverb, that is suitable in construction industry. The proverb illustrates how important it is, to fix arrangements and agreements in a written form. The same applies for ARGE agreements.

This survey argues that the ARGE is form requiring. Indeed there is the possibility that Partnerships under Civil Law could be founded by implication and conclusive acting, but it must be recommended to conclude a partnership agreement. When there is not an ARGE agreement which defines suitable conditions, obligation and liabilities, the partnership is a Partnership under Civil Law concerning legal aspects. Law takes other regulations than contractual arrangements. In ARGE agreement could be defined other regulations than in law. Relating to insolvency, could be defined that the ARGE has to continue business with the remaining partners. Another example is the limitation of liability. In relation to the principal are ARGE partner jointly and several liable, but in internal relationship could be defined other regulations.

ARGE has the purpose to fulfil the contract for work. For the ARGE partners, the partnership has the purpose to reach maximum profit coupled with moderate efforts. The ARGE partners are not interested in providing the best personal they have. Usually, the ARGE has not only the name of one partner. In most cases the ARGE name is coupled to the project. Therefore partners are not afraid about damaging their reputation. They use their good qualified employees for accomplishing the own contracts. Therefore the ARGE agreement has to define the services which have to be accomplished in relation to the several partners.

Advantages of ARGE are recognizable from the perspective of the principal. He has one contractual partner and gets services from one hand. Behind his contractual partner, the ARGE, are concealed several engineering firms which are responsible and liable for accomplishing the project. The principal shifts his responsibility for coordination and project management to the architects and planners. Investors and builder do not want to be responsible for interfaces between planners.

[238] German proverb: „Wer schreibt, der bleibt".

The ARGE partnership has fundamental disadvantages for engineering firms. In the legal form of Partnership under Civil Law, partners are jointly and several liable. Liable for services they are not competent for. Inherent to this liability is an incalculable risk. Incalculable risk, due to principals claims for damages.

In general, the step before founding an ARGE is a tendering partnership. Partners have to be aware of signing a written pre-contract or tendering agreement. After successful tender procedure, leads the pre-contract to the ARGE agreement. The ARGE agreement has to be arranged before signing the contract for work with the principal. The same theory applies: recording is rewarding.

13 Bibliography

13.1 Literature

Bärwaldt, Roman (2002): Beck'sches Handbuch der Personengesellschaften §17, 2nd Edition, Beck juristischer Verlag, 2002.

Boldt, Antje (2005): Der neue Bauvertrag, 2nd Edition, Carl Heymanns Verlag KG Köln 2005.

Buchhardt, Hans-Peter; Pfülb, Wolfgang (1998): Kommentar zum ARGE und Dach-ARGE-Vertrag, 3rd edition, Bauverlag GmbH Wiesbaden und Berlin, 1998

Devonshire-Ellis, Chris; Scott, Andy; Wollard, Sam (2011): Setting up Joint Ventures in China, 3rd edition, Springer Verlag Berlin Heidelberg 2011.

Garbes, Michael (2008): Die Haftpflichtversicherung der Architekten/Ingenieure, 3rd edition, Verlag Versicherungswirtschaft GmbH, Karlsruhe 2008.

Giefers, Hans-Werner; Ott, Hans (2000): Die Gesellschaft bürgerlichen Rechts, 4th edition, Rudolf Haufe Verlag GmbH & Co. KG Freiburg, Berlin 2000.

Häußermann, Daniel; Heisenberg, Julia; Knacke, Jürgen; Theilig, Andreas (2008): Praxiswissen Baurecht für Architekten und Ingenieure; Verlag W. Kohlhammer, Stuttgart 2008.

Heiermann, Wolfgang; Riedl, Richard; Rusam, Martin (2008): Handkommentar zur VOB, 11th Edition, Vieweg + Teubner Wiesbaden 2008.

Hueck, Götz; Windbichler, Christine (2008): Gesellschaftsrecht, 21th edition, Verlag C.H. Beck München 2008.

Jagenburg, Inge; Schröder, Carsten U. (2008): Der ARGE-Vertrag; 2nd Edition, Werner Verlag Köln 2008.

Krause-Allenstein, Florian (2007): Die Bau-ARGE–Haftung, Sicherheiten, Versicherungen im Innen- und Außenverhältnis, Journal Baurecht, Volume: 38, No. 4 pages 617 – 631.

Lang, Fritz; Mulansky, Katja; Mulansky, Thomas (2010): Die Gesellschaft bürgerlichen Rechts, Schäfer – Poeschel Verlag Stuttgart 2010.

Lang, Volker (2000): Die BGB – Gesellschaft und die Partnerschaft, 2nd edition, Deutscher Sparkassenverlag GmbH Stuttgart 2000.

Leimböck, Egon; Iding, Andreas (2005): Bauwirtschaft, Teubner Verlag 2nd edition, Wiesbaden 2005.

Locher, Horst; Koeble, Wolfgang; Frik, Werner; Locher, Ulrich (2010): Kommentar zur HOAI, 10th edition, Werner Verlag 2010

Messerschmidt Burkard; Thierau, Thomas (2007a): Die Bau-ARGE. Teil 1: Grundstrukturen und Vertragsgestaltung NZBau 2007, page 129 et seq.

Messerschmidt Burkard.; Thierau, Thomas (2007b): Die Bau-ARGE. Teil 2: Die Dach-ARGE insbesondere NZBau 2007, S. 205 et seq.

Mütze, Michael; Senff, Thomas; Möller, Jutta C. (2007): Real Estate Investments in Germany, Springer Verlag Berlin Heidelberg 2007.

Noorwood, Stephen R.; Mansfield, Nigel R. (1999): Joint Ventures issues concerning European and Asian construction markets of the 1990's, International Journal of Project Management Vol. 17, No. 2, pp. 89-93, Elsevier Science Ltd and IPMA Great Britain 1999.

Palandt, Otto.; Sprau, Hartwig (2008): Bürgerliches Gesetzbuch – Kommentar, 67th edition, Beck Juristischer Verlag München 2008.

Schwarz, Karl (2007): Probleme bei einer Bau-ARGE und einer Bauherren-ARGE – Rechtnatur, Insolvenz eines Gesellschafters und Sicherheit nach §648a BGB, article from ZfBR Zeitschrift für deutsches und Internationales Bau- und Vergaberecht, 30 No. 7, 2007, page 636 – 642.

Simmendinger, Heinz (2009): HOAI 2009; Ernst und Sohn Berlin 2009.

Wirth, Axel; Würfele, Falk; Broocks, Stefan (2004): Rechtsgrundlagen des Architekten und Ingenieurs; 1st Edition; Friedr. Vieweg & Sohn Verlag / GWV Fachverlage GmbH Wiesbaden 2004.

Ulmer, Carsten; Schäfer, Peter (2009): Gesellschaft bürgerlichen Rechts und Partnergesellschaft, 5th Edition, C.H. Beck Nördlingen 2009.

13.2 Other sources

BBR – Besondere Bedinungen und Risikobeschreibungen für die Berufshaftpflichtversicherung von Architekten, Bauingenieuren und Beratenden Ingenieuren, Musterbedingungen des GDV, 2007

Chamber of Architects in Baden-Württemberg (2005): Arbeitsgemeinschaftsvertrag, 2005

Federal Statistical Office Germany (2011): Finanzen und Steuern 2009, Wiesbaden 2011.

Gauch, Peter (1982): Probleme von und mit Subunternehmern, Festschrift Meier-Hayoz Bern 1982.

German Civil Code (BGB) in the version promulgated on 2 January 2002 in Federal Law Gazette, last amended by statute of 28 September 2009.

Insolvency Statute of Germany (InsO) in the version promulgated on 19.10.1994, last amended by statute of 21.10.2011.

Kieß, Daniela (2012): Tax consultant at Ellinger & Rückle Leinfelden-Echterdingen, interview.

Model Contract of German Construction Industry Federation (2005): Joint Venture Agreement, Version 2005, Wibau Holding und Service GmbH, Düsseldorf.

Müller, Mario (2012): CEO of Müller & Bleher Filderstadt GmbH + Co. KG, Interview.

13.3 Internet

URL: http://www.baunetz.de/recht/BGH_bestaetigt_Bezugnahme_auf_Leistungsbilder_oder_Leistungsphasen_der_HOAI_fuehrt_zu_entsprechender_Leistungspflicht_44766.html, date: 27.01.2012.

URL: http://bgb.jura.uni-hamburg.de/av/gesellschaftsrecht/bgb-g.htm, date 06.01.2012.

URL: http://www.brennecke-partner.de/110164/Das-Recht-der-GbR-Teil-5-1-Wechsel-der-Gesellschafter, date 07.02.2012.

URL: http://www.buergschaft24.de/tl_files/BB24/Vertragsbeziehungen-in-der-kautionsversicherung.jpg, date: 28.01.2012.

URL: http://www.business-services.fraport.de/content/fraport_ag_business-services/de/misc/binaer/bewerber-_bietergemeinschaftserklaerung/jcr:content.file/bewerberbietergemeinschaftserklaerung_pl.pdf, date: 08.02.2012.

URL: http://bwi-bau.de/fileadmin/daten/pdf/Argeformen.pdf, date 05.02.2012.

URL: http://www.existenzgruender.de/selbstaendigkeit/vorbereitung/gruendungswissen/rechtsform/05/index.php, date 07.02.2012.

URL: http://www.foerderland.de/2101.0.html, date 29.12.2012.

URL: http://www.frankfurt-main.ihk.de/english/business/legal_forms/gbr/, date: 31.12.2011.

URL: http://www.gesetze-im-internet.de/gewstg/__2a.html, date: 04.01.2012.

URL: http://guide.theemiratesnetwork.com/living/business.php , date 07.02.2012.

URL: http://www.hk24.de/recht_und_fair_play/steuerrecht/steuerexi_ordner/366794/ Gesellschaft_buergerlichen_Rechts_Gruendung_und_Steuern.html;jsessionid= B4B748D723111FA80E7809B4C0F65425.repl21#10, date: 06.02.2011.

URL: http://www.steuernetz.de/ aav_steuernetz/lexikon/K-10646.xhtml?currentModule=home, date: 07.02.2012.

URL: http://www.stuttgart.ihk24.de/recht_und_fair_play/Gesellschaftsrecht_ Unternehmensformen/Wahl_der_Rechtsform-Gesellschaftsrecht/971294/ Aufloesung_GmbH.html;jsessionid= 8B1E2A5DB441469EDF68A3D7C 3C55376.repl23#8, date 07.02.2012.

URL: http://ted.europa.eu/ udl?uri=TED:NOTICE:28746-2012:TEXT:DE:HTML&src=0, date 05.02.2012.

URL: http://ted.europa.eu/udl?uri=TED:NOTICE:42398-2012:TEXT:DE: HTML&src=0, date: 08.02.2012.

URL: http://www.uni-marburg.de/fb01/studium/zusatzqualifikation/privates_baurecht /vorlesunge /baurecht_materialien/ws0607_materialien/baurecht_messerschmidt/ ws0607_baurecht_arge0, date: 08.02.2012.

14 List of Jurisdiction

BGH (1974): Judgement from 07.03.1974 - VII ZR 217/72, in BGHZ 62, 204.

BGH (1997), judgement from 15.05.1997 – VII ZR 287 /95, in BauR 1997, 1018.

BGH (1999): Judgement from 12.07.1999 - II ZR 4/98, in BauR 1999, 1471.

BGH (2001): Judgement from 29.01.2001 – II ZR 331/00, in NJW 2001, 1056.

BGH (2003): Judgement from 07.04.2003 – II ZR 56/02, in NJW 2003, 1803

BGH (2007): Judgement from 26.07.2007 - V II ZR 42 / 05, in BGHZ 173, 314.

OLG Frankfurt (1981): Judgement from 27.05.1981 – 17 U 82/80, in BauR 1983, 156.